Arrows Words 1

1	2	3
14	15	16

Grid clues:

- have a strong effect
- Neandertal's disappeared
- it opposes the thought
- people employed by one organization
- bind or compel someone
- soap for washing the hair
- part of a play
- cessation of war or violence
- individual thing or person regarded as single
- really
- employment
- the outside limit of an area
- up to one point in time
- launch, cast
- lighthearted pleasure
- granular substance, pale yellowish
- Creator
- remain, or be kept in a specified state
- private police that guards building, park..
- wire that conveys electric current
- put something more
- at least a small amount or number
- used with approximately quantity
- sound that is loud or unpleasant
- become longer
- basic unit of an element
- former
- person who is studying at a school
- seed-bearing head of a cereal
- it is drawn into the lungs
- request someone to do or give
- provide booklet giving a list of items at an event
- possess
- used to introduce a negative statement
- frozen mixture of fruit juice and sugar
- with a mattress and coverings
- method of human communication
- part of a tree that grows out from the trunk
- it has points on all its faces

© Dupuis Logiciels

Arrows Words 2

1	2	3	4	5	6	7	8	9	10	11	12	13
14	15	16	17	18	19	20	21	22	23	24	25	26

give out a bright light

some are considered as a pest

get as far as

present again for further consideration

men of a particular nation

laid by a female bird

person who works in a school

associated with the people easily identified.

of an identical type is played with notes

in the middle of

article

in accordance with the rules, legitimate

remain secure in position

used before the first of two alternatives

not easily broken, bent, or pierced

procedure for accomplishing

large, heavy, mammal

move rhythmically to music

speed sports competition

by every one of a group

theater figure

worked by electricity

move about in a hurried way

accept his responsibilities

it emits from a station

behind, following

action taken to achieve a purpose

properly positioned so as to be level, upright

little man

request for dissatisfaction

chief in size or importance

color as an overcast sky.

the taste of the beautiful

part connecting the head to the body.

thin piece of wood used to light a fire

© Dupuis Logiciels

Arrows Words 3

1	2	3	4	5	6	7	8	9	10	11	12	13
14	15	16	17	18	19	20	21	22	23	24	25	26

Clues in grid:

- plane figure with three straight sides and three angles
- over and not touching
- people of the same age
- large sheet of salt water
- one's father
- rate at which something is able to move
- before the expected time
- educate, instruct
- it can be bank
- the totality
- investigate systematically
- bar used to hang things on
- of considerable importance
- come near or nearer
- at this moment, now
- regardless of
- Take with you
- distinct from a human being
- possibility of harm or injury
- in accordance with (9,2)
- located a short distance away
- look at and comprehend the meaning of written matter
- between him and me
- cylindrical metal container
- in a suitable state for an activity
- the watchman must not close it
- it symbolizes a state of America
- hearts, spades, clubs and diamonds
- small vessel propelled on water
- eat sparingly to lose weight.
- star around which the earth orbits
- word by which a person is known
- action in a series taken to achieve a thing.
- sprinkle water over a plant
- they go from shoulder to hand

© Dupuis Logiciels

Arrows Words 4

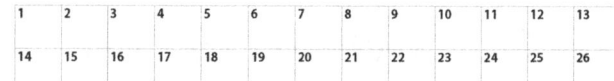

1	2	3	4	5	6	7	8	9	10	11	12	13
14	15	16	17	18	19	20	21	22	23	24	25	26

Arrows Words 5

1	2	3	4	5	6	7	8	9	10	11	12	13
14	15	16	17	18	19	20	21	22	23	24	25	26

not the same as another or each other

having a large amount of excess flesh

the wealth and resources of a country

make something less severe

be a candidate in an election

which is out of the ordinary

cessation of movement or operation

electrical appliance not functioning

with little or no light

small number of

numerical adjective

make the flow difficult or impossible

all the rooms on the same level

may be enforced by penalties.

School transportation

behind one

defeat the enemy

on all occasions

we stay there when we are sick

seeking carefully and thoroughly.

region of the atmosphere

arrange for the delivery by mail

choice by vote

swallow to feed

decision to be taken

of a newspaper unscrupulously sensational

a short time ago

retain possession of

arrange for someone to sit

food containing spices

there, we learn every day

strip of material worn around the collar and tied in a knot

pass away

the main section of a plane

medical practitioner

covering of paint laid on a surface

write on a typewriter or computer

© Dupuis Logiciels

Arrows Words 6

1	2	3	4	5	6	7	8	9	10	11	12	13
14	15	16	17	18	19	20	21	22	23	24	25	26

Grid clues:

- used before a family name (5,4)
- the last word of the tale
- distinguished by its atomic number
- pieces making up the skeleton
- it's a choice
- state of wanting to know or learn
- gain a point in a competitive game
- as of blood, fire, or rubies.
- feeling fear or anxiety
- the product of three and three
- acquire knowledge
- the little one has just arrived
- portion of an object or of material
- its detector reveals the truth
- used to single out one over all others
- it arrives with the command
- at some time in the past
- the first one is childhood
- state of affairs, set of circumstances
- procedure for making extra copies
- belonging to or associated with us
- which presents different aspects
- distinct from one already mentioned
- important thing that happens
- a word that leads to another
- as a result or consequence of this
- is to exploit when it is great
- used to refer to all the members
- habitually or typically occurring or done
- journey made on horseback, on a bicycle
- start an action or activity
- decide for yourself
- fruit always green
- length or portion of time
- period when being as a visitor or guest.

© Dupuis Logiciels

Arrows Words 7

1	2	3	4	5	6	7	8	9	10	11	12	13
14	15	16	17	18	19	20	21	22	23	24	25	26

have an effect on	in addition	upper limb of the human body	essential element in a sports team	1	2	3	4	4	the beginning of something	not exposed to danger or risk
3	who is partisan	3	2	4	5	6	extremely unpleasant, and degrading	7	8	4	7
9	5	10		easy to perceive, understand	3	group of students who are taught	11	procedure to verify the quality or reliability	3	way people are connected	3	place at a higher level
9	he knows how to make himself obey	12			1	2	8	3	10		9	
8		6	that pleases the eye	13		1	element of the forest	7	10	8	8
1	13	14	8	9		7	ice crystals and falling in light white flakes	8		2
7	point awarded for a correct answer	3		5	not us, but them	find a solution to	4	5	2	15	8
elevation of the earth's surface rising abruptly	12	5	16	17	7	3	14	17		3		15
	3		7		13	not at home or at one's place of work	5	16	7		3
7	10	3	14	3		8		18		14	
person undergoing training for a particular job	19		9		10	where an incident in life or fiction occurs	length of strong cord	10	5	20	8
	suppose without being sure	21	16	4	4		having the power, skill, means	17	small domesticated carnivorous
		2	clothing for a particular purpose		1	forming a foundation or starting point	6	3	4	14	1
15	word used to describe an action	circular object that revolves on an axle	18	13	8	8	2		13		3
8	discern, deduce mentally after reflection	4	8	8		17	be part of reality	8	22	14	4	7
10	in days gone by		3		8			20	
6	8	9	3	10	8				

© Dupuis Logiciels

Arrows Words 8

1	2	3	4	5	6	7	8	9	10	11	12	13
14	15	16	17	18	19	20	21	22	23	24	25	26

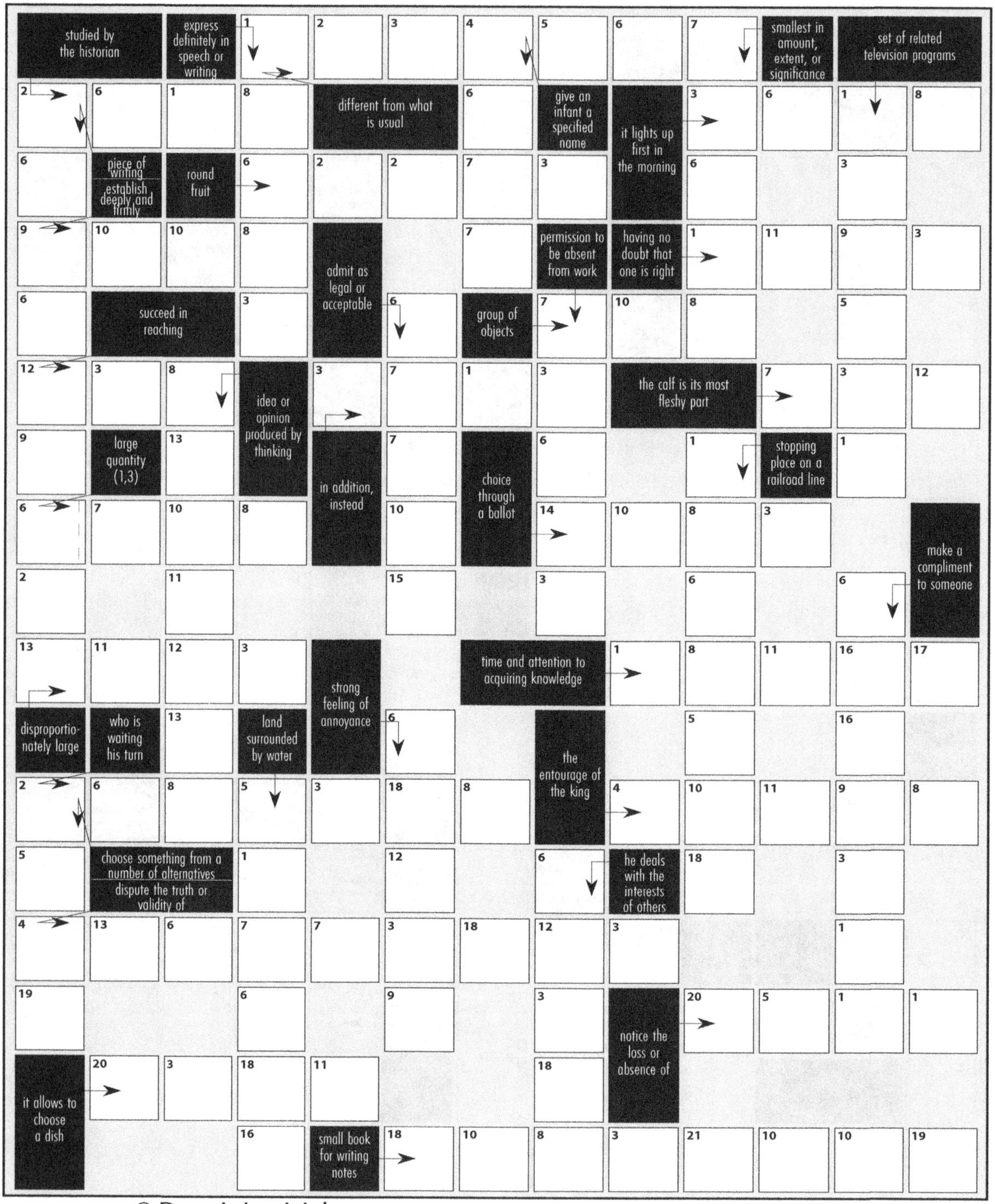

A grid puzzle with the following clues placed in cells:

- studied by the historian
- express definitely in speech or writing
- smallest in amount, extent, or significance
- set of related television programs
- different from what is usual
- give an infant a specified name
- it lights up first in the morning
- piece of writing, establish deeply and firmly
- round fruit
- admit as legal or acceptable
- permission to be absent from work
- having no doubt that one is right
- succeed in reaching
- group of objects
- idea or opinion produced by thinking
- the calf is its most fleshy part
- large quantity (1,3)
- in addition, instead
- choice through a ballot
- stopping place on a railroad line
- make a compliment to someone
- time and attention to acquiring knowledge
- disproportionately large
- who is waiting his turn
- land surrounded by water
- strong feeling of annoyance
- the entourage of the king
- choose something from a number of alternatives
- dispute the truth or validity of
- he deals with the interests of others
- notice the loss or absence of
- it allows to choose a dish
- small book for writing notes

© Dupuis Logiciels

Arrows Words 9

1	2	3	4	5	6	7	8	9	10	11	12	13
14	15	16	17	18	19	20	21	22	23	24	25	26

color produced by mixing red, yellow, and black	person who is hostile		1	2	1	3	4	5	6	1	a reaction to a question
7	3	8	9	10	activity to improve health and fitness	11	person considered to be the same in status	12	become different	13	material extended on a mast to catch the wind	13
13	of poor quality	be in the leading position on	physical and sports in college	1	14	15	4	13	16	5	8	10
14	perhaps represents everything for her	12	5	17	branch of a tree that has been cut off	13	10	18	6
asking for information specifying something		1	19	18	8	20	the girl we are talking about	worrying because of possible danger	9
9	12	13	16	13	gladly receive what is given	1	6	12	1
13	indicate that one is eagerly impatient	14	thing that is wanted or required	4	to hold stably	1	1	3
5	the total of things in number	which is essential	10	1	4	1	6	6	13	3	19
16	13	21	1	detailed proposal for achieving something	1	16	it flows in pipelines	5	nearly	13
undertake, or perform an action or task	17	1	22	18	13	10	8	5	18
9	8	3	14	16	brittle substance transparent	7	hit the ball to begin play	15	17
single element of speech or writing	15	1	power to provide light and heat	20	18	13	6	6	8
5	10	23	1	10	16	5	1	exactly the same	6
develop, innovate	16	(of the wind) cool and fairly strong	1	public road in a city or town	6	16	3	1	1	16
		24	3	1	6	12	23	23
perform a task (5,3)		20	number of days of the week	6	1	23	1	10
4	13	3	3	19	8	15	16	10

© Dupuis Logiciels

Arrows Words 10

1	2	3	4	5	6	7	8	9	10	11	12	13
14	15	16	17	18	19	20	21	22	23	24	25	26

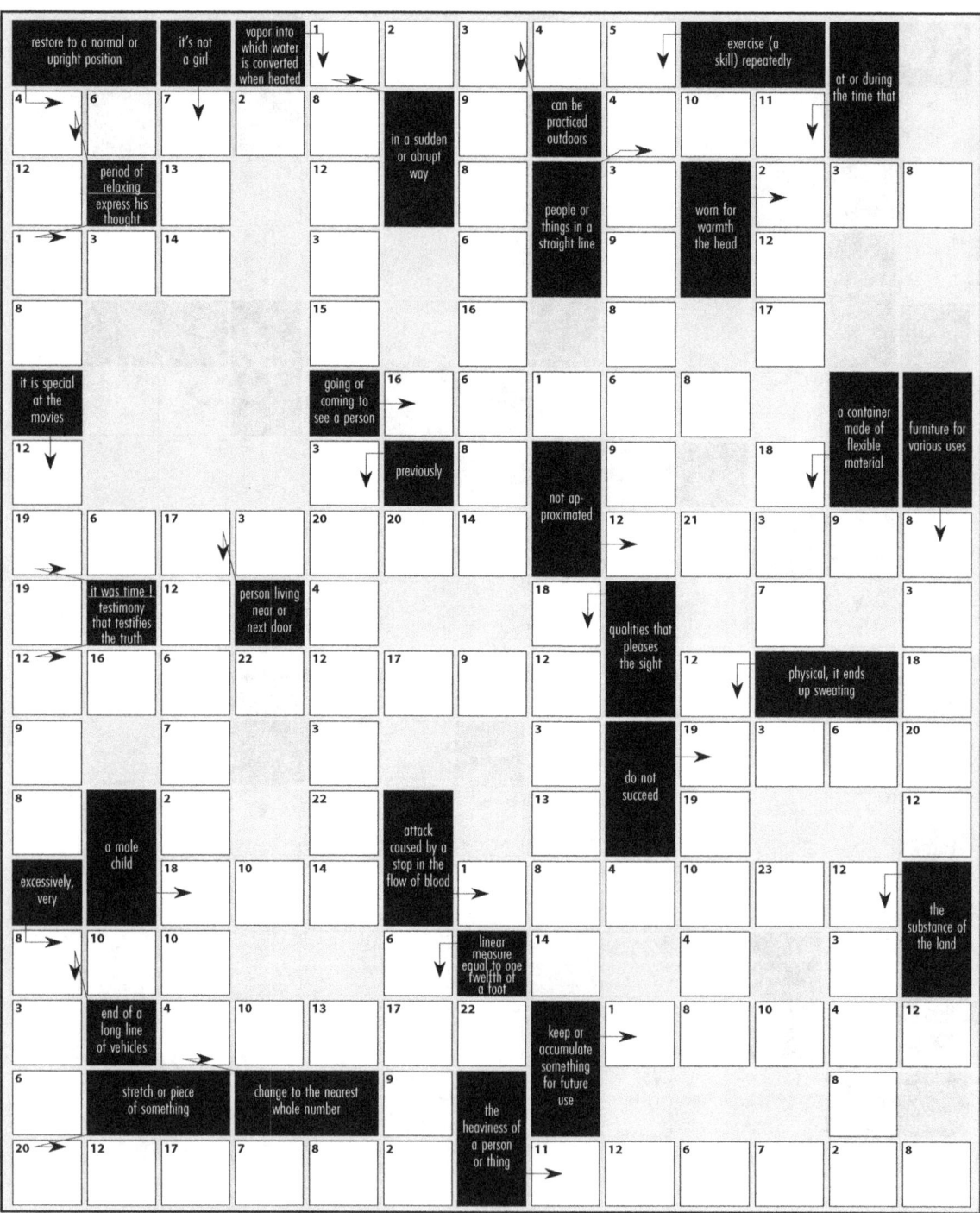

© Dupuis Logiciels

Arrows Words 11

1	2	3	4	5	6	7	8	9	10	11	12	13
14	15	16	17	18	19	20	21	22	23	24	25	26

© Dupuis Logiciels

Arrows Words 12

1	2	3	4	5	6	7	8	9	10	11	12	13
14	15	16	17	18	19	20	21	22	23	24	25	26

give someone something they want	particular way of considering something	organize	1	2	3	4	5	6	stir in all directions	move at a regular and fairly slow pace
7	5	8	9	3	used to express uncertainty	5	move to a higher position	the way in which	4	9	10
5	popular trend in styles of dress get some shut-eye	11	2	11	6	1	2	5	13	12
6	12	2	2	1	say to convey an opinion, or a feeling	6	1	2	5	13	12
4	10	5	2	start to exist	2	13
11	make an attempt or effort to do something	14	3	15	5	16	in the US the day after Thanksgiving, special offers by retailers
9	5	the chief must demonstrate it	2	1	12
17	9	18	17	universal knowledge	1	5
word used to identify	relating to the body as opposed to the mind	14	2
propel the body through water	4	15	6	11	19	5	12	19
6	statement that indicates a danger	9	19	3	adhere or cling to a substance or surface	13
10	5	3	17	11	17	20	imposing in appearance, or style	6	7
11	11	2	going back to a place or activity	3	2	14	18	3	17	propane or butane
21	14	no longer alive	17	5	11	it gives the paw to its master	11
15	19	17	19	22	9	20
22	2	5	22	13	5	mark the agreement	5
15	2	6

© Dupuis Logiciels

Arrows Words 13

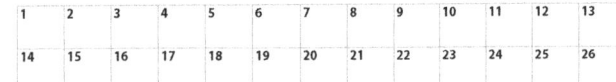

1	2	3	4	5	6	7	8	9	10	11	12	13
14	15	16	17	18	19	20	21	22	23	24	25	26

information acquired by a person	describe the importance of something	it is at the lowest for the sea	give an account in words	after the first in time or order	1	2	3	4	5

5	6	3	7	8	9	10	11	9	capital raised by a business through shares.	12	better to draw the good one

9	that of the riddle is rarely in the pocket	13		9		9		4	shed tears	4	13	14

14	disagreement between two or more groups	10	15	16	15	1	15	3	6	10

armed struggle		9		9		4		6	1	graduated range of values for measuring

7	12	13		8	make smaller in amount, degree, or size	13	9	10	17	4	9

12	stone structure that divides an area of land	failure of electrical supply	18		15	it's not true	situated at a great distance		12	the way in which one acts	18

8	come up by using feet and hands	4	8	15	19	18		20	12	8	1	9

8		12		perceive with the ear	9	make a sketch	12		9		21

no problem of end of the month	13	15	4	21		bare or lacking adornment	10	13	14		12

take something away or off		5	associated with a female person	21	9	13	large musical instrument having rows of tuned pipes			16

13	9	19	3	16	9		12			having a friendly nature	15

9	say again something repeated / decorative design	condition under an agreement is reached	17	12	operate or function, especially properly	7	3	13	5		3

22	12	2	2	9	13	6	which comes right after	13	15	13

9	consent to do something	9	machine that converts power into motion	9	6	11	15	6	9

12	11	13	9	9	23	12	10

2	19	hard, solid, nonmetallic mineral	1	2	3	6	9

© Dupuis Logiciels

Arrows Words 14

1	2	3	4	5	6	7	8	9	10	11	12	13
14	15	16	17	18	19	20	21	22	23	24	25	26

© Dupuis Logiciels

Arrows Words 15

1	2	3	4	5	6	7	8	9	10	11	12	13
14	15	16	17	18	19	20	21	22	23	24	25	26

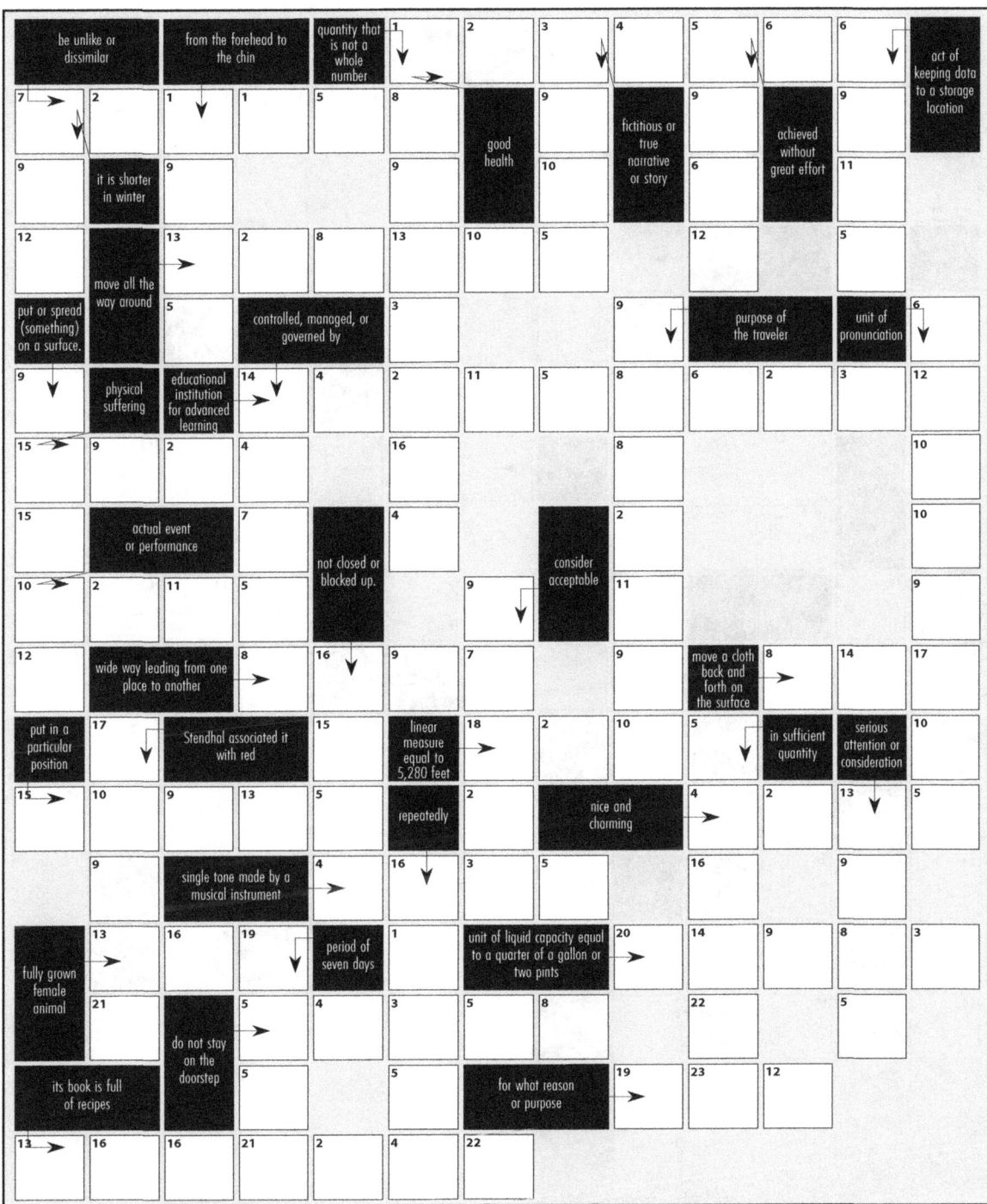

Arrows Words 16

1	2	3	4	5	6	7	8	9	10	11	12	13
14	15	16	17	18	19	20	21	22	23	24	25	26

having the qualities required	1	2	3	4	4	informal gathering, by a club or group.	giving a sense of happy enjoyment	appear to move below the earth's horizon	despite the fact that
vegetation cultivated on lawns	5	6	part of a play	5	7	7	5	4	8	9	10
7	5	4	9	on the other side of a specific area	6	11	10	12
position of paid employment	13	it is indicated by an arrow	13	8	2	10	6	9	8	5	14
3	put in more individual feature, fact, or item	3	basic unit of an element	happening immediately	3	3	each of the sections of the zodiac	thing deposited as a guarantee	15
13	10	9	3	8	11	4	4	8	1	14
13	coherent, large body of matter with no definite shape	5	14	fixed price charged for something	2	3	9	10	12
more than sure	16	3	4	4	14	quantity with which measures could be done	6	people employed by one organization	4
17	where flowers and plants are grown	9	9	15	14	8	9
6	10	2	9	3	8	14	symbol denoting a number	2	3
be aware of through information	13	release from captivity	14	15	14	9	8	11	18
19	used to introduce a negative statement	18	8	9	up to one point in time	16	9	18
14	5	2	be of the right shape and size for	great weight	12	10	3	20	21	object that sounds a clear musical note when struck
5	seed-bearing head of a cereal	10	3	2	part of house	2	transparent crystalline solid	8	17
22	10	upper layer of earth in which plants grow	5	a separate clause of a legal document	2	2	9	8	6	11	10
		4	5	8	11				10	11
		16								11

© Dupuis Logiciels

Arrows Words 17

1	2	3	4	5	6	7	8	9	10	11	12	13
14	15	16	17	18	19	20	21	22	23	24	25	26

The grid clues are as follows:

- human beings considered collectively
- a comb separates them
- considered in proportion to something else
- he goes to the competition
- citizen of a particular country
- swaying or oscillation of a ship
- result of an operation
- characteristic of the United States
- celestial body moving around a star
- to the greatest extent
- it becomes more lively at altitude
- supply a machine with material, power
- existing as a result of birth
- it distinguishes the male and the female
- the most forward part of something
- thing that is discussed in the space separating
- with the others
- graphite used as the part of a pencil
- the outside limit of an area
- person who works in a school
- group or party favoring socialist
- perform a surgical operation
- article
- music, painting or cinema
- express gratitude
- as regards, in relation to
- serve someone with food or drink
- formal address to an audience
- it is neither right nor left
- person who prepares food
- of an identical type
- laid by a female bird
- human being regarded as an individual
- up until the present

© Dupuis Logiciels

Arrows Words 18

1	2	3	4	5	6	7	8	9	10	11	12	13
14	15	16	17	18	19	20	21	22	23	24	25	26

boy in relation to his parents

contain as part of a whole

by every one of a group

category of things or people

grow in intensity

support from one place to another

convergence of views

large sheet of salt water

they go from shoulder to hand

bind or compel someone

an occupation undertaken for a signifi-cant period

with a great deal of effort

it advances in the summer

the totality

group opposing another in a dispute

before any pronominal verb

granular substance, pale yellowish

used as a friendly form of address

its shot gives the start

it is part of the bestiary

throughout a period of time

fixed luminous point in the night sky

it has points on all its faces

its line is indispensable

large, heavy, mammal

take a seat

he is part of the siblings

appointed to act or speak for someone

the watchman must not close it

refer to something that is extre-mely strong

group of notes sounded together

line produced on paper or cloth by folding

journey by a vehicle on a regular basis

account of an act kept in writing

cultivated plant that is grown as food

nothing more besides

single specimen of a book or publication

one's father

Arrows Words 19

1	2	3	4	5	6	7	8	9	10	11	12	13
14	15	16	17	18	19	20	21	22	23	24	25	26

The grid contains the following clues:

- we read it in the waiting room
- on the subject of, concerning
- small animal that has six legs
- flowering plant's unit of reproduction
- movements that match the rhythm of the music.
- pay out in buying or hiring goods
- used to refer to a thing, no matter how many
- apparatus using or applying mechanical power
- before the expected time
- think carefully before making a decision
- introducing a subordinate clause
- twelve o'clock in the day
- the house of the Lord
- product of five and two
- to be, it is to fight
- place of business
- earlier (after a measurement of time)
- number smaller than ten
- literary man
- belonging to the people previously mentioned
- feeling of great pleasure
- it's warming up on the bed
- to the highest degree
- made of cardboard, for storing papers
- marriage ceremony
- betray, abandon
- the subway system in London
- cylindrical metal container
- employment
- continue for a specified period of time
- person who shows the way to others
- it is the subject of a contract
- verbal or written answer
- request someone to do or give

Arrows Words 20

1	2	3	4	5	6	7	8	9	10	11	12	13
14	15	16	17	18	19	20	21	22	23	24	25	26

Clues appearing in the grid:

- it emits from a station
- very far from the surface
- part of the land near the sea
- written after investigation apply pressure to
- natural disposition
- appearing or hero
- it opposes the thought
- really
- at the present time
- Creator
- thing likely to cause damage or danger
- between him and me
- defeat the enemy
- obstruction blocking a hole
- it is grown in the countryside
- mathematical ratio
- human habitation
- after that
- is equal to two and two
- of a liquid relatively firm in consistency
- get as far as
- decision to be taken
- make something less severe
- outcome
- in soccer kick the ball to score a goal
- management of money
- where goods or services are sold
- layer of tissue covering of the body
- we use it when we go out
- the wealth and resources of a country
- pass away
- not strict or sufficiently strict

© Dupuis Logiciels

Arrows Words 21

1	2	3	4	5	6	7	8	9	10	11	12	13
14	15	16	17	18	19	20	21	22	23	24	25	26

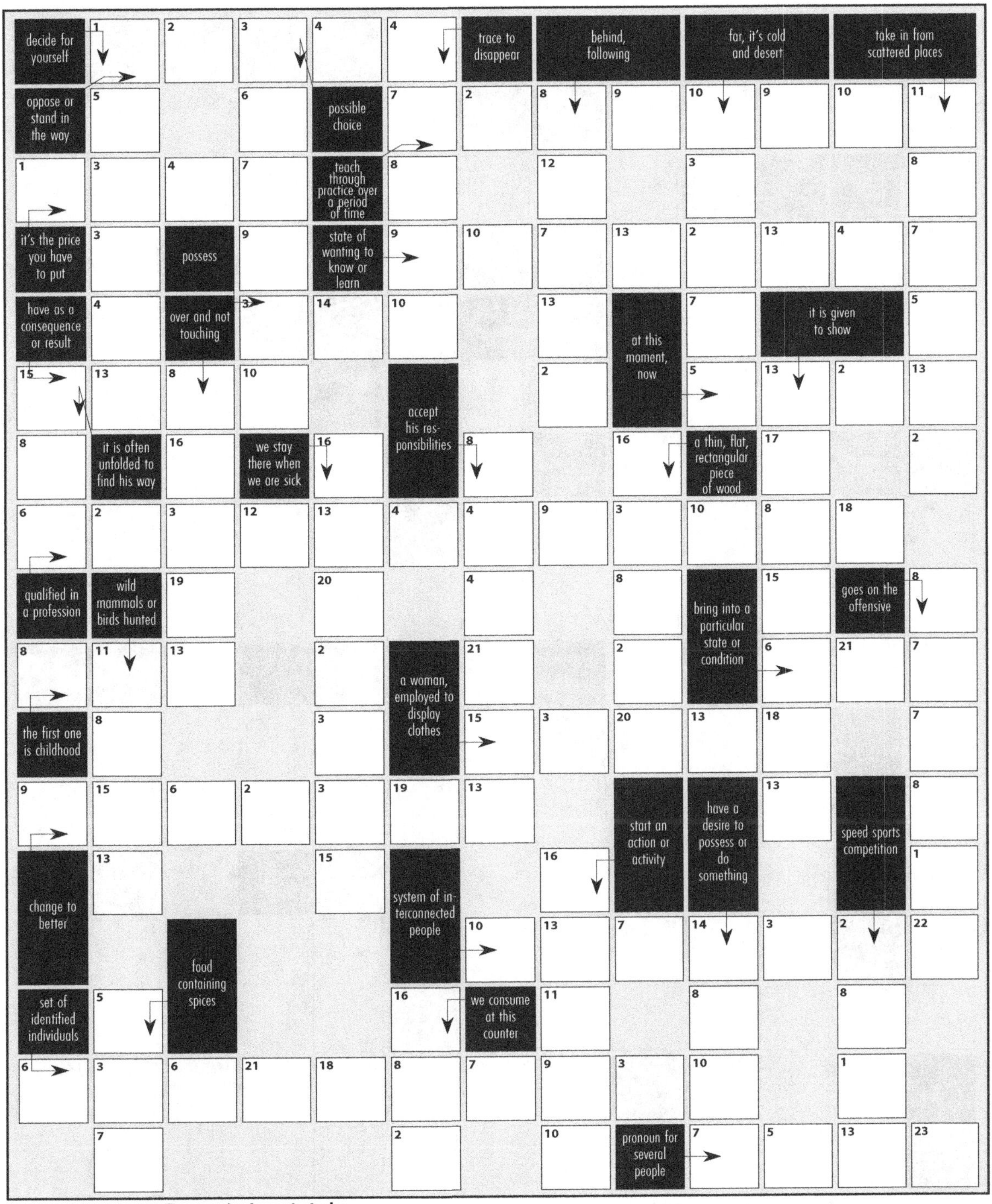

decide for yourself	1	2	3	4	4	trace to disappear	behind, following	far, it's cold and desert	take in from scattered places

(grid puzzle)

© Dupuis Logiciels

Arrows Words 22

1	2	3	4	5	6	7	8	9	10	11	12	13
14	15	16	17	18	19	20	21	22	23	24	25	26

place or fix an object		maintain an upright position		1	2	3	4	system of ideas intended to explain something	money paid to someone for work		worked by electricity	
5	3	6	7	4	particular place or point	take place	8	9	2	2	10	7
9	when teams compete series of railroad cars	public service	having the power, skill, means	9	11	12	10		9		12	
4	13	9	14	7	forms about 20 percent of the earth's atmosphere		3	15	16	17	10	7
18		19		19	male ruler of an independent state		13	way or track laid down for walking	lacking sufficient money to live		18	
8	3	5	10	region of the atmosphere	1	20	16		2	9	4	8
institution for people needing care	reference to someone or something	14		11	of considerable importance	14	it is projected on the screen		3		13	
5	10	7	4	14	3	7		5	3	21	14	10
9	cloth or fabric / try out	14		17		17			13		18	
4	10	1	4		rate at which something is able to move		11	it arrives with the command		9	for the one who is not satiated	
10	supporter of the conservative Party	4		1			14			17		
13		13	10	2	6	11	12	14	18	9	7	
14	used to indicate the existence of something	9		10			12	slope built used for launching and landing boats		14	the smallest unit of an organism	18
9		4	8	10	13	10	for the reason that; because	1	14	7	18	10
12		14		19				12				12
who is partisan	22	3	13	person holding public office	3	22	22	14	18	14	9	12
	7							2				

© Dupuis Logiciels

Arrows Words 23

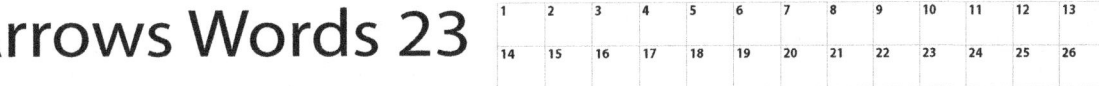

1	2	3	4	5	6	7	8	9	10	11	12	13
14	15	16	17	18	19	20	21	22	23	24	25	26

Grid clues:

- have an effect on
- make one's living by growing crops or keeping livestock
- sudden movement of surprise
- polite or old-fashioned form for woman
- different from what is usual
- used to single out one over all others
- is to exploit when it is great
- depending on (7,2)
- area regarded as remote
- round fruit
- unit of measurement of angles
- the extent or measurement of a surface
- small vessel propelled on water
- material object representing something abstract
- chronological record of public events
- choice by vote
- set of related television programs
- use as a point from which something can develop.
- nocturnal mammal capable of flight
- names written one below the other.
- it triumphs when the error disappears
- unit of linear measure equal to 3 feet
- part of the dollar
- not us, but them
- interrogative pronoun
- appeal to his imagination
- which is out of the ordinary
- belonging to or associated with us
- give out a bright light
- meet someone socially or by chance
- writers, artists, sharing similar ideas, style.
- cessation of movement or operation
- small round portion of liquid

© Dupuis Logiciels

Arrows Words 24

destroy by friction or use	period of time now occurring	1	2	3	4	5	6	3	look at written words	substantial in size, number, or quality
7	6	2	3	person taking part in an undertaking with anothers	6	explain to someone how to do something	in addition, instead	6	8	9	6
10	be successful or victorious	6	It is a pet catching mice	11	2	4		2		6	
5	12	10	9	6	sword or rifle	11	with little or no light	13	2	3	14
sound that is loud or unpleasant	possibility of something happening	6	asking for information specifying something	7	15	2	4	condition that someone is in at a time	10	
11	15	2	5	11	6		be or allow to be visible	9	15	12	7
2	useful to film / adult human male	4	he deals with the interests of others	2	16	6	5	4		17	to the point of surpassing or exceeding
18	2	5	located a short distance away	1	distinguished by its atomic number	in addition	2	8	9	12
6	basic monetary unit of Brazil	6	brief period of time	18	12	18	6	5	perform services for another person	17
3	6	2	8		5		8	it lights up very early in the summer	6	9	4
2		3		communist during the Cold War	3	6	13	adult human female	6	
method of human communication	19	little man	excellently	19	behind one	18	fairly or comfortably high temperature	7	3	18
8	2	5	16	17	2	16	6	12		20	
people, or things having common characteristics	19	3	11	quantity, but not necessarily quality	5	17	18	19	6	3
4	21	1	6	14	4		2			
persist in an activity	2		provoke displeasure, or hostility	2	5	16	6	3
11	12	5	4	10	5	17	6			

© Dupuis Logiciels

Arrows Words 25

1	2	3	4	5	6	7	8	9	10	11	12	13
14	15	16	17	18	19	20	21	22	23	24	25	26

come near or nearer	likely to happen		state of being connected		feeling fear or anxiety	we sit there	1	2	3	4	5		person or thing that is different
6	7	7	8	3	6	1	9		end of a period of time or activity		1	sequence of action in a play, movie	3
monetary unit of the US	8	5		10		gladly receive what is given	6	1	1	5	7	11	
12	3	2	2	6	8		13	who touches the world		14		9	
	15		6	reach a place at the end of a journey	6	8	8	13	16	5		5	
7	6	8	11		13			14			familiar acquiescence		8
some but not all of something	15	productive- ness, hard work	13	14	12	17	4	11	8	18		present, and future regarded as a whole	
in the middle of	2		3		including a great variety of people or things			5	lunch or dinner	5	6	11	
	5	the little one has just arrived	14	5	19			8		6		13	
6	when it is good it is effective		4	chemical element of atomic number 26	13	8		14	can represent everything for her	9	13	20	
20	5	11	9	3	12			6				5	
3			13	the substance of the land	5	6	8	11	9		period when being as a visitor or guest.		
14			7		at some time in the past		13	of poor quality	15		4		
21	5	11	which can be combined with a vowel to form a syllable	1	3	14	4	3	14	6	14	11	
succeed in reaching	especially great or intense				14			14		12		6	
7	6	8	11	13	1	17	2	6	8			18	
				5			2						

© Dupuis Logiciels

Arrows Words 26

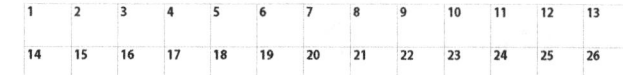

1	2	3	4	5	6	7	8	9	10	11	12	13
14	15	16	17	18	19	20	21	22	23	24	25	26

Grid clues:

- fundamental work for the scientist
- added at the end of a word to form another one
- welcome a visitor
- a call to take part in a competition
- strong cabinet with a complex lock
- sit on a horse or a bike problem
- showing stylish excellence
- electrical appliance not functioning
- offspring, of an animal before or soon after birth
- acquire knowledge
- combine or put together to form one substance
- being the same in quantity
- must be taken to win
- exactly the same
- color intermediate between black and white
- the main section of a plane
- come after a person or a thing
- fruit always green
- procedure for making extra copies
- small number of
- circular object that revolves on an axle
- is never the last word of the sentence
- take charge of business
- its detector reveals the truth
- person who is hostile
- musical ensemble
- device held in the hand
- it flows in pipelines
- exceed an amount, level, or number
- general color of a piece of writing, situation
- in addition, also
- soap for washing the hair

© Dupuis Logiciels

Arrows Words 27

1	2	3	4	5	6	7	8	9	10	11	12	13
14	15	16	17	18	19	20	21	22	23	24	25	26

A crossword-style arrow words grid with the following clues:

- policeman
- experience strongly
- live for a time in a tent
- actual use as opposed to theories
- used to express uncertainty
- supply of money that can be provided
- white crystalline substance that gives seawater
- perceive and register when water is heated
- size that is less than normal
- as a result or consequence of this
- see and spend time with someone
- egg-laying vertebrate able to fly
- it is special at the movies
- he knows how to make himself obey
- small part of something
- it comes after the conclusion
- together the locals
- a solid or hollow sphere
- the moment of the serenade
- stopping place on a railroad line
- having a pH greater than 7
- a container made of flexible material
- can be practiced outdoors
- it is sometimes tight
- refer to things belonging to
- continuing toward completion of a task
- upper limb of the human body
- propane or butane
- an eccentric or unusual person
- put one leg in front of the other in walking

© Dupuis Logiciels

Arrows Words 28

1	2	3	4	5	6	7	8	9	10	11	12	13
14	15	16	17	18	19	20	21	22	23	24	25	26

bring to a lower state, condition, or role	ten years of life	in a suitable state for an activity `1`	`2`	`3`	`4` `2`	`5`	`6`	qualities that pleases the sight

The grid clues include:

- bring to a lower state, condition, or role
- ten years of life
- in a suitable state for an activity
- qualities that pleases the sight
- think deeply or carefully about
- last game in a competition
- make something has happen
- remain or be left
- assistant, in particular
- world collectively, including plants, animals, the landscape
- nearly
- it is sleeping in its basket
- large body of water
- small book for writing notes
- the one we are talking about
- intimate or botanical
- financial record
- fact of being with others
- apply a substance shaped like a circle
- being the only one of its kind
- direction taken by summer visitors
- the product of three and three
- pieces making up the skeleton
- hearts, spades, clubs and diamonds
- is played by the orchestra
- device for measuring time
- take place
- a road vehicle with four wheels
- a male child
- effort to accomplish something
- ensure accuracy
- number of poles
- nation
- only to you

© Dupuis Logiciels

Arrows Words 29

something that is not curved or bent		a pair is forming a railroad track		concerning all or most people		alloy of iron with carbon	2	3	3	4	a sheet to read
1	5	6	7	8	9	10	5		11	7	
3	look to be a charge against the defendant	7			3		3	be in the arms of Morpheus	12	9	physical and sports in college
3	13	8	11	3	14	15	3		15	3	
16		2	follow the course or trail of someone or something	3		2		7	an organized scheme or method.	1	
that pleases the eye	17	word to describe a thing or to express a concept	5	3	6	16	detailed analysis of a subject or situation	1	5	12	11	18
18	3	7	6		7	the total of things in number	17	surround an object with a strip	8		1
the new begins at the end of the previous	7		7		2		7	16	19	12	14	5
20	12	8	15	21	near the end of a period	14		14		3	
doing something in a short time	5		21	former	19	2	11		a reaction to a question	16	
10	8	5	17	the product of a thousand and a million	7		7	7	is ready to fight	
dose of a psychoactive drug	22	book that lists the words	11	8	15	5	8	19	14	7	6	18
15	12	5	2	3	sign of operation	1	16	
divide into pieces with a knife	2	move through the air	22	2	18	attorney or counselor	2	7	23	18	3	6
				8		3		3	11	
18	3	2	2	19	23	having no doubt that one is right	1	12	6	3
color between green and orange			14		1	

© Dupuis Logiciels

Arrows Words 30

Grid clues:

- perceive with the ear
- organize
- be fixed or unable to move
- distinct section of a piece of writing
- event, or other thing that occurs again
- undergo natural development
- assemble something from individual parts
- place of care vessel larger than a boat
- the condition of having paid work
- end of a long line of vehicles
- develop, innovate
- moderately high degree
- thing that unites or links people
- at any time
- it can make credit
- a short time ago
- not moving or making a sound
- part connecting the head to the body.
- smallest in amount, extent, or significance
- which may be possible
- set of outer clothes consisting of a jacket and trousers
- make sounds and that are of lively amusement
- group of objects
- the calf is its most fleshy part
- alight on the ground
- naming word
- habitually or typically occurring or done
- the degree of excellence of something
- construct something large
- it's not a girl
- move a cloth back and forth on the surface
- large amount
- land surrounded by water
- become longer

© Dupuis Logiciels

Arrows Words 31

1	2	3	4	5	6	7	8	9	10	11	12	13
14	15	16	17	18	19	20	21	22	23	24	25	26

frozen mixture of fruit juice and sugar	permission to be absent from work	1	2	3	4	5	3	action of buying and selling	number of musketeers of A.Dumas	get up from lying, sitting
6	7	4	taking place near the end	8	despite the fact that	preferably	9	2	3	8	4	9
10	create by the mind	3	11	10	2	8	6
2	basic unit of an element	12	meteorological conditions	13	make a compliment to someone	2	14	14	9	4	5	5
15	4	15	used before the first of two alternatives	4	4	a separate clause of a legal document	4
6	word by which a person is known	at or during the time that	16	8	4	17	high temperature	8	4	2	3
17	2	10	4	6	situation under consideration	9	to face the other way	2
4	satisfied with his fate	part of a play	2	7	3	10	2	3	3	4	9
worn for warmth the head	8	2	3	seed-bearing head of a cereal	8	it sometimes goes beyond fiction	6	11
2	8	4	2	9	7	13
2	18	18	4	2	9	4	detailed proposal for achieving something	18	1	2	17
become visible	18	9	compulsory contribution to state revenue	3	2	19	4	14
propel the body through water	20	shed tears	21	with a mattress and coverings	1	5	faculty of perceiving odors	4	do not stay on the doorstep
5	earth, together with all of its countries	7	set of manufacturing objects	4	22	13	6	18	10	4	17	3
16	11	9	1	14	3	4	3
6	20	small piece of metal to fit in a lock	23	4	20	1	4
10	1	9

© Dupuis Logiciels

Arrows Words 32

1	2	3	4	5	6	7	8	9	10	11	12	13
14	15	16	17	18	19	20	21	22	23	24	25	26

article

act of seeking for someone or something

move in a specified direction

physical suffering

we put the cutleryr there

formal address to an audience

presenting few difficulties

a specialist

consent to do something

in the direction of... give way to anxiety

consider acceptable

percentage basis

common to or characteristic of a nation

action such as to produce a particular effect

negro-spiritual

no longer alive

the outside limit of an area

used to introduce a negative statement

purpose of the traveler

thing that can be seen

his coming is a pleasure for the seller

place at a higher level

liquid as refreshment or nourishment

cut into pieces perform a surgical operation

bare or lacking adornment

important thing that happens

sound produced in a person's larynx

covering for the foot, typically made of leather

information in the form of a graph, or diagram

fulfill a commitment

worst is its opposite

food made of flour and water

Arrows Words 33

1	2	3	4	5	6	7	8	9	10	11	12	13
14	15	16	17	18	19	20	21	22	23	24	25	26

Arrows Words 34

1	2	3	4	5	6	7	8	9	10	11	12	13
14	15	16	17	18	19	20	21	22	23	24	25	26

The grid below is an "Arrow Words" (arrowword) puzzle. The clues appear inside the shaded cells, pointing to the answer cells.

Clues in the grid:

- large, heavy, mammal
- denoting the most important
- large sheet of salt water
- disproportionately large
- announce an explanation
- brittle substance transparent
- by every one of a group
- wire that conveys electric current
- employment
- large piece of stone not closed or blocked up.
- request someone to do or give
- very large expanse of sea
- used with approximately quantity
- record an incident or fact
- consisting of two identical
- person connected by blood or marriage
- it allows to choose a dish
- one-piece garment for a woman
- bind or compel someone
- opposite to the face
- a price asked for goods or services
- agreement by two or more parties
- it gives the thrill
- it's not true
- the watchman must not close it
- it is to learn before playing
- poet or musician
- parry the blow
- it's a young lady
- consuming a material such as coal or wood
- laid by a female bird
- cylindrical metal container
- controlled, managed, or governed by
- mass of vapor floating in the sky
- its shot gives the start
- grow in intensity

© Dupuis Logiciels

Arrows Words 35

1	2	3	4	5	6	7	8	9	10	11	12	13
14	15	16	17	18	19	20	21	22	23	24	25	26

The grid is an arrow-words (fléchés) puzzle with the following clues placed in shaded cells:

- plates protecting the skin of fish
- convergence of views
- add salt, herbs, pepper to food
- get as far as
- that which is morally right
- power to provide light and heat
- talented performer in movies or sports
- machine that converts power into motion
- provide group of words
- put clothes on, dress
- put something more
- release from captivity
- defeat the enemy
- small pear-shaped fruit with sweet dark flesh
- offer to carry out work or buy land, shares..
- oneself, in particular
- for preserving food at very low temperatures.
- it ends up blowing and sweating
- people employed by one organization
- result of an operation
- except, apart from
- individual thing or person regarded as single
- value according to a particular scale
- thing such as a chair or stool
- natural oily or greasy substance
- product of five and two
- large quantity (1,3)
- row of written or printed words
- number of faces of a dice
- for nothing in the world
- collapse
- associated with a female person
- degree or intensity of heat
- pass away
- inanimate object distinct from a living being

© Dupuis Logiciels

Arrows Words 36

1	2	3	4	5	6	7	8	9	10	11	12	13
14	15	16	17	18	19	20	21	22	23	24	25	26

relating to the present	move rhythmically to music	move slowly and carefully	**1**	**2**	**3**	**4**	**5**	**2**	**4**	amount of something gained or acquired
6	**7**	**8**	**9**	**10**	**2**	happening immediately	**7**	arrange in groups according to type, class	**2**	whichever of might be chosen	**5**
9	piece of music — stretch or piece of something	**5**	person who works in a school	support from one place to another	**11**	**5**	**10**	**10**	**12**	between him and me	**13**	of an identical type
14	**9**	**2**	**15**	**4**	**16**		**4**	commitment ceremony	permission granted	**12**	**9**	**3**
7	it is given to show	**11**		**9**	put in an application for	**5**	question to know the person	**17**	**16**	**7**		**5**
8		**9**	**18**	**5**	**6**	**19**	**14**	**9**		**20**		**6**
12	some are considered as a pest			**11**		**19**	we use it when we go out	**8**				**9**
having a great deal of money or assets	**10**	**1**	**11**	**16**		**14**		**8**	**7**	**7**	**10**	justification for an action or event
dry, barren area of land	**2**		**9**		**12**		**1**			**9**	
8	**9**	**3**	**9**	**10**	**4**	with deep, dense, or heavy mass	**5**	**2**	**1**	**6**	**5**	**14**
9	draw and create feeling of confidence	**9**		**16**		distinct from a human being	**15**	number of points achieved in a game		**3**	
3	**9**	**11**	**20**	**10**	**1**	**4**	**12**	not prompt to understand	**3**	**14**	**7**	**17**
1	**4**	toward, or relating to one side	**11**		where a person may arrange to receive letters		**11**	**2**	
15	having similar qualities or characteristics	**14**	**1**	**13**	**9**		**21**	**7**	**18**	
2	**1**	**11**	**9**			make something less severe	**10**	
nice and charming	side of a ship that is on the left	all the rooms on the same level	**22**	**14**	**7**	**7**	**10**	**9**	**5**	**3**	**9**
19	**7**	**10**	**4**				

© Dupuis Logiciels

Arrows Words 37

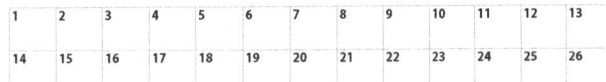

1	2	3	4	5	6	7	8	9	10	11	12	13
14	15	16	17	18	19	20	21	22	23	24	25	26

having the power, skill, means	unit of measure equal to 12 inches	(of the wind) cool and fairly strong	trace to disappear	1	2	3	4	5	the wealth and resources of a country	follow as the consequence of something
3	place to quench your thirst	6	5	5	7	expanse that is free, available	8	to be, it is to fight	4	3	9	5
10	3	9		the reverse of someone or something	3	earlier (after a measurement of time)	3	8	11	serious attention or consideration	5
12	in or after a short time	5		13		13	used for breathing and smelling	14	11	1	5
5		1	11	14		14	easily understood or done	11	15
	16	2	verbal or written answer		1	13	17	2	12	5
suppose without being sure	activity with physical exertion and skill	1	2	11	9	7	18	7
	10	we stay there when we are sick	11	he distributes the mail	5	accept his responsibilities	3	have a strong effect	13	contain as part of a whole	13
8	15	5	1	1	2	11	1	7	17	3	14
coming before all others	19	13	12	1	2	4
6	13	9	1	7	18	young branch springing from a tree	15	an instance of a disease	3	12
3	situated at a great distance	11	5	17	4	15
9	11	11	17	choose the best or most suitable	1	5	12	5	4	7	19
part of house	17	16	3	5
framework, arrangement of something complex.	teacher of the highest rank	2	9	11	6	5	1	1	11	9	people or things in a straight line
		11	5	11
1	7	9	15	4	7	15	9	5	possess	11	20	14

Arrows Words 38

1	2	3	4	5	6	7	8	9	10	11	12	13
14	15	16	17	18	19	20	21	22	23	24	25	26

used to indicate the existence of something	produce energy or activity	where a prisoner is locked up	1	2	3	4	5	3	choice by vote		used to single out one over all others
6	**7**	**3**	**2**	**3**	line produced on paper or cloth by folding	**1**	it opposes the thought	**8**	**9**	**10**	**3**
4	story that is imaginatively recounted, regional	**11**	continue for a specified period of time	**8**	**4**	**5**	**6**	actual event or performance	**3**		**5**
8	**12**	**1**	**4**	**8**	like the German or American state		**9**	cultivated plant that is grown as food	**1**	**2**	**12**	**13**
3		**9**	foremost line of an armed force	**14**	**2**	**12**	**15**	**6**		**3**
hard seed in a cherry, plum, peach	**5**	**6**	**12**	**15**	**3**	**15**	**9**	**1**
16	one's father	**3**	be situated in a particular place	**16**	who is partisan	**14**	**12**	**2**	**9**
4		rectangular piece of paper	**5**	**7**	**3**	**3**	**6**	associated with the people easily identified.	**15**	the part on which it rests or is supported.	**4**
16	**9**	**3**	**6**	the first one is childhood	**2**	**7**		**17**	**8**
kinds of food habitually eaten	have as a consequence or result		**4**	**4**	**18**	**3**	do not succeed	**14**	**4**	**9**	**8**
19	**3**	**4**	**15**	the beginning of something	**8**	period of seven days	**9**	those (article)	**5**		**20**
4	the majority of — take a seat	used in expressions with an exception or contrast	**16**	literary man	**21**	**2**	**9**	**6**	**3**	**2**	speed sports competition
5	**9**	**6**	discern, deduce mentally after reflection	**5**	**3**	**3**	cessation of war or violence	**7**	**4**
5	food containing spices	**7**	**12**	**6**		**3**	**13**	**3**	**4**	**1**	**3**
boy in relation to his parents		**4**		**4**	**22**		**19**		**3**
5	**12**	**15**		**2**
	plan of action to achieve a major aim	**5**	**6**	**2**	**4**	**6**	**3**	**18**	**20**

© Dupuis Logiciels

Arrows Words 39

1	2	3	4	5	6	7	8	9	10	11	12	13
14	15	16	17	18	19	20	21	22	23	24	25	26

Arrows Words 40

1	2	3	4	5	6	7	8	9	10	11	12	13
14	15	16	17	18	19	20	21	22	23	24	25	26

The grid clues:

- succeed in reaching
- express definitely in speech or writing
- colored substance that is spread over a surface
- call someone on the telephone
- the ace or the king or the Queen
- cessation of movement or operation
- come near or nearer
- cows floor
- it's a choice
- not us, but them
- worked by electricity
- period when being as a visitor or guest.
- place of management of a company
- he deals with the interests of others
- keep a supply available for sale.
- great weight
- familiar acquiescence
- swallow to feed
- the end of the life
- a device for recording visual images
- at the highest point
- in days gone by
- also (2,4)
- in the middle of
- keep or accumulate something for future use
- belonging to or associated with us
- which is out of the ordinary
- perhaps represents everything for her
- where an incident in life or fiction occurs
- in accordance with fact or reality
- consult it to prepare an itinerary
- series of actions taken to achieve a goal
- official list or register of names

© Dupuis Logiciels

Arrows Words 41

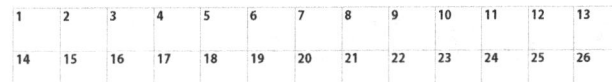

1	2	3	4	5	6	7	8	9	10	11	12	13
14	15	16	17	18	19	20	21	22	23	24	25	26

it is covered with scales	armless seat	1	2	3	4	3	1	5	6	4	moisture condensed from the atmosphere that falls
7	8	9	2	appearing or hero	1	in accordance with (9,2)	10	round fruit	of considerable importance	3	
3	can be hidden behind a mask	gladly receive what is given	3	1	6	10	5	11	8	12	
1			8	13	14		names written one below the other.		15	must be taken to win	
6		the decision-making body of a company	4	4	in addition, instead	6	14	9	6	before the expected time	3
occasionally, rather than all of the time	11		not approximated	16		8	co-ordinating conjunction	3	15	16	
9	13	17	6	5	8	17	6	9	4	18	
plane figure with three sides	3	19	15		5	14	3				
5	4	8	3	15	12	14	6	person who is hostile	20	15	
previously	16	division of a unit	1	exercise authority over people	5	the little one has just arrived	15	6	21	including a great variety of people or things	5
3	its detector reveals the truth	9	5	4	13	22	6	is to exploit when it is great	8	16	6	3
14	8	6	act of hitting someone or something	23	twelve o'clock in the day	17	16		12	
4	area under control of another country	1	13	14	13	15	20	6	6	
6		5	6	13			flow or cause to flow (liquid)		
3	unload a passenger on the way	8	think carefully before making a decision	1	13	15	9	8	16	6	4
16	4	13	10		15		23	
20	15		key to move the carriage of a typewriter back	4	6	5	23	4	15

© Dupuis Logiciels

Arrows Words 42

1	2	3	4	5	6	7	8	9	10	11	12	13
14	15	16	17	18	19	20	21	22	23	24	25	26

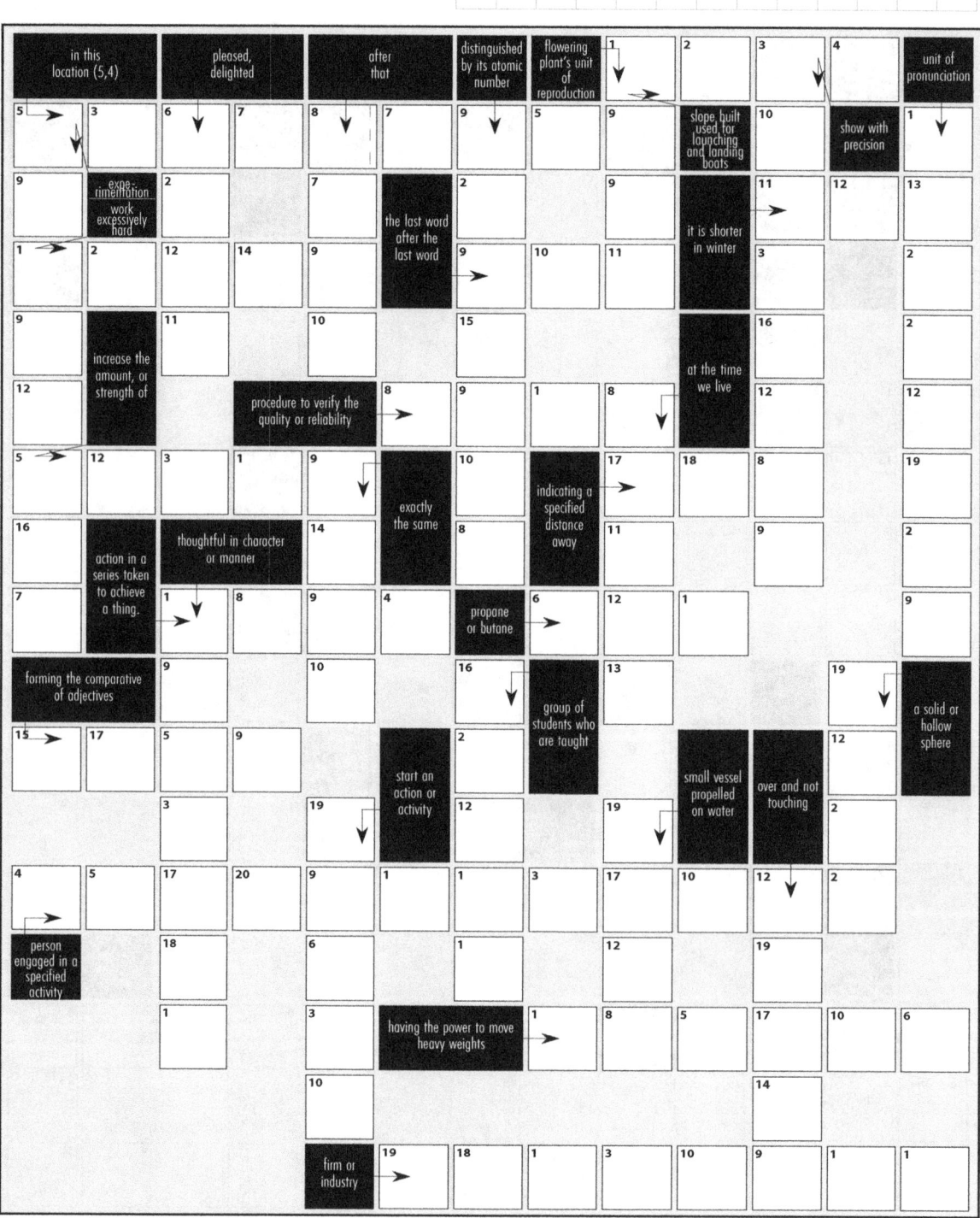

© Dupuis Logiciels

Arrows Words 43

1	2	3	4	5	6	7	8	9	10	11	12	13
14	15	16	17	18	19	20	21	22	23	24	25	26

military fight

exercise (a skill) repeatedly

a comb separates them

piece of work to be done

as a result or consequence of this

ten years of life

way or track laid down for walking

natural disposition

expressive of enthusiasm move gently to and fro

supply of money that can be provided

give one's attention to a sound

distinct from one already mentioned

live for a time in a tent

look at and comprehend the meaning of written matter

equal to the product of two and ten

sound that is loud or unpleasant

have an effect on

the place or situation in which

policeman

the product of three and three

vapor into which water is converted when heated

the substance of the land

upper limb of the human body

brief period of time

in the mouth of one who is not satisfied

strong feeling of annoyance

electrical appliance not functioning

made of cardboard, for storing papers

only to you

used to refer to two people or things

converse or communicate by spoken words

life-supporting component of the air

little man

make your choice

small in size, amount, or degree

colour next to orange and opposite violet

© Dupuis Logiciels

Arrows Words 44

1	2	3	4	5	6	7	8	9	10	11	12	13
14	15	16	17	18	19	20	21	22	23	24	25	26

The grid clues:

- become unable to find
- supply a machine with material, power
- stopping place on a railroad line
- used before a family name (5,4)
- cease work in order to relax
- fixed period for which something lasts
- we read it in the waiting room
- mother tongue / be necessary
- used to refer to all the members
- properly positioned so as to be level, upright
- the beginning of the night
- qualities that pleases the sight
- it arrives with the command
- intimate or botanical
- considerable great size
- worse than usual, of a low quality.
- expresses himself emotionally
- last game in a competition
- a reaction to a question
- take part in a sport
- operate a place or one equipment
- medical practitioner
- Collective action
- give the impression of being something
- it is achieved when we have succeeded
- from a higher to a lower point
- single tone made by a musical instrument
- the girl we are talking about
- only one, not one of several
- thickened skin on the toes
- hand tool for cutting wood
- direct attention by extending one's finger.
- person considered to be the same in status

Arrows Words 45

Grid clues:

- invite someone to engage in a contest
- the total of things in number
- the calf is its most fleshy part
- together the locals
- part of the dollar
- small domesticated carnivorous
- number of poles
- figure, formed by two short intersecting lines
- he puts the team in condition
- be of use in achieving or satisfying
- it ends up with a breakdown
- action or process of thinking
- they do not all have the same duration
- equal corresponding parts
- place of business
- land and its buildings used for growing crops
- device performing a particular task
- refer to things belonging to
- former
- make an attempt or effort to do something
- group of people with a common interest
- universal knowledge
- the main section of a plane
- change to better
- bold and vivid colors
- facts provided or learned
- take place
- morally good, or acceptable
- basic monetary unit of Brazil
- it flows in pipelines
- expressing trajectory across an area
- everyone is obliged to comply with it

© Dupuis Logiciels

Arrows Words 46

1	2	3	4	5	6	7	8	9	10	11	12	13
14	15	16	17	18	19	20	21	22	23	24	25	26

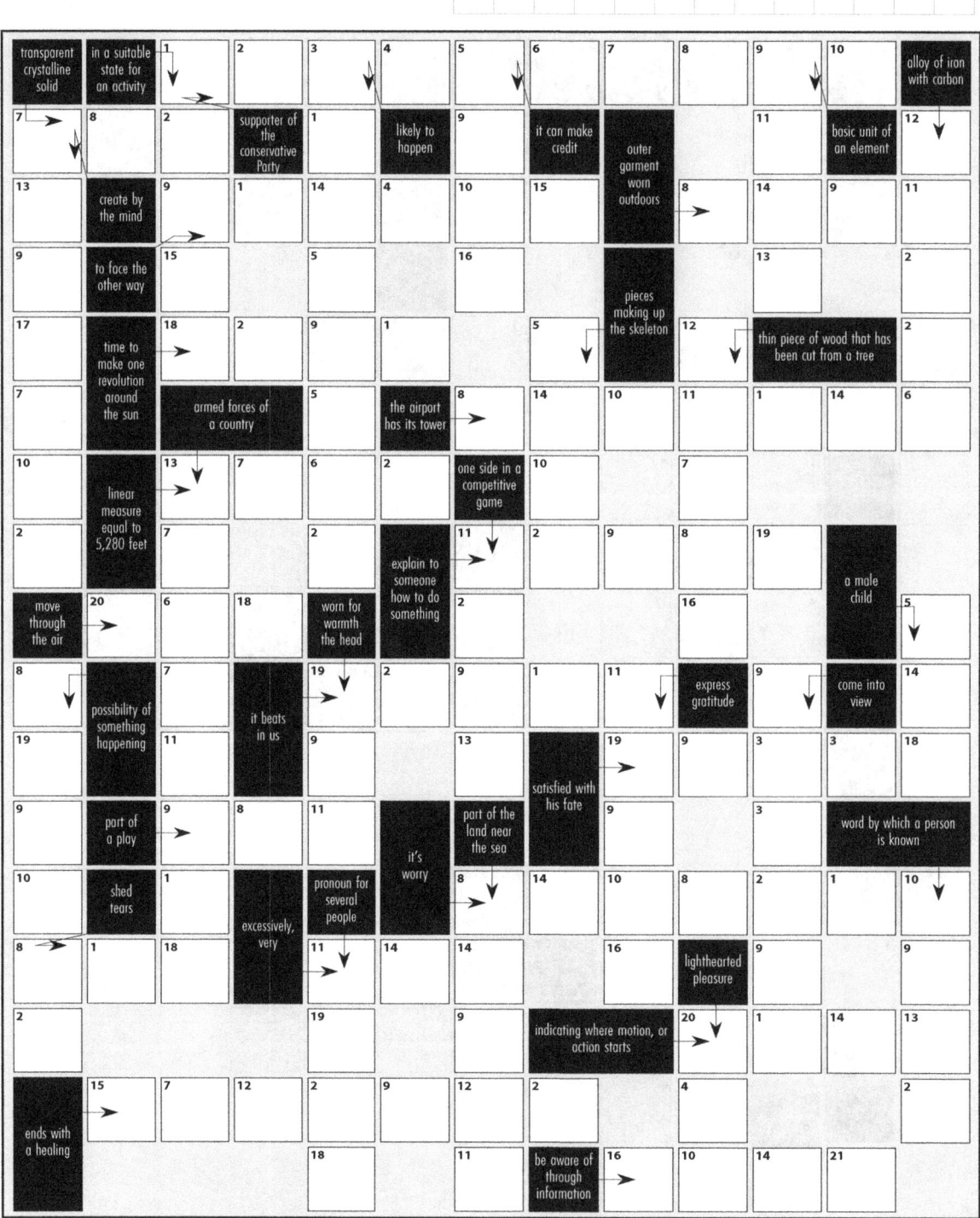

Arrows Words 47

1	2	3	4	5	6	7	8	9	10	11	12	13
14	15	16	17	18	19	20	21	22	23	24	25	26

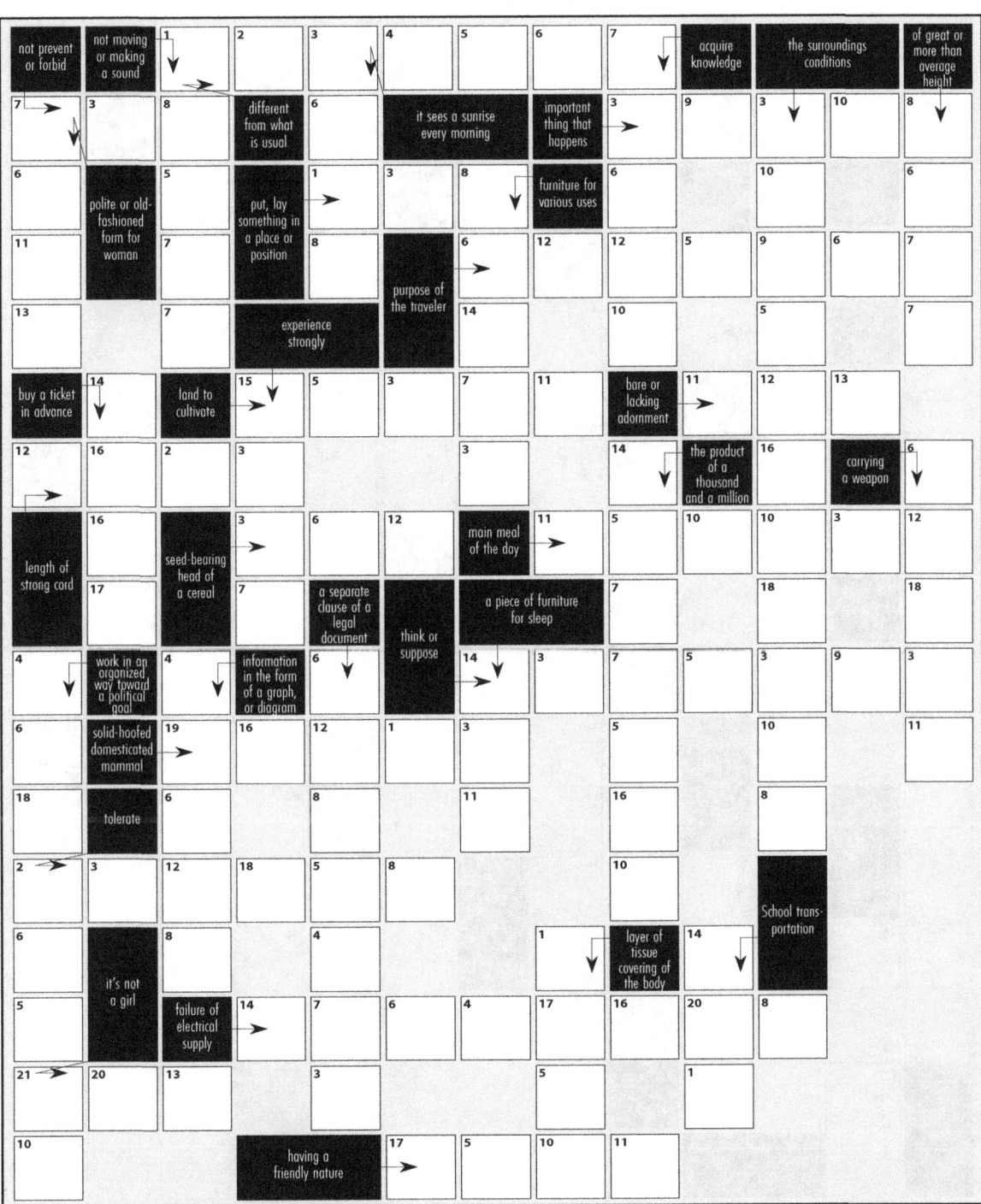

© Dupuis Logiciels

Arrows Words 48

1	2	3	4	5	6	7	8	9	10	11	12	13
14	15	16	17	18	19	20	21	22	23	24	25	26

we say that the sea one is pure	hair become this color with age	1	2	3	4	4	bring a person under one's control by force.	long, hollow cylinder of metal or plastic			large body of water	events told for en-tertainment
3	5	2	vegetation cultivated on lawns	6	feeling fear or anxiety	7	8	9	5	10		4
11	management its first is a holiday	3	move a cloth repeatedly back and forth on the surface	2	7	12	up to one point in time	7	music, painting or cinema	3	2	9
13	3	14		it is the subject of a contract	15	16	12	17	16
5	used to introduce a negative statement	cause or allow someone or something to have	1	5	18	19	19	19	2
8	16	2	state of things as they actually exist	11	soap for washing the hair	20	12	that pleases the eye	14
5	seeking carefully and thoroughly.	19		person who is studying at a school	4	9	7	11	19	8	9	end of a long line of vehicles
4	19	3	2	20	21	is played by the orchestra	3	3
9	bar used to hang things on	10	combine or put together to form one substance	3	13	7	4	5	20
2	3	5	10	13	5	22	9	10
3	9	with a great deal of volume	23	make a sketch	5	consider acceptable
9	he gets the rent	14	10	16	7	11	6	3
5	object that sounds a note when struck	12	16	change to the nearest whole number	2	16	7	8	11
16	24	8	19	2	article	3	10	13
8	10	is generally larger than a village and smaller than a city	9	16	24	8	5
the totality	3	10	10	21	9
	atmosphere as regards heat, dryness, sunshine, wind, rain	24	19	3	9	21	19	2

© Dupuis Logiciels

Arrows Words 49

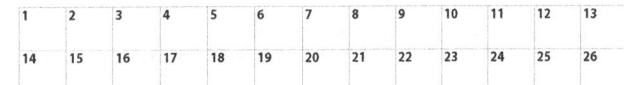

1	2	3	4	5	6	7	8	9	10	11	12	13
14	15	16	17	18	19	20	21	22	23	24	25	26

provide funding for

citizen of a particular country

which is essential

large sheet of salt water

organize

individual feature, fact, or item

after all attention, observation

suffix denoting a quality or condition

event, or other thing that occurs again

we must take it only by being sober

give a spoken or written account of something

bear all or part of the weight of

compulsory contribution to state revenue

on all occasions

follow the course or trail of someone or something

behind, following

is equal to two and two

write on a typewriter or computer

nearly

action such as to produce a particular effect

at any time

group of houses larger than a hamlet and smaller than a town

plenty of it on the beach

we take it by daring

small number of

employment

set of words with subject and verb

Arrows Words 50

1	2	3	4	5	6	7	8	9	10	11	12	13
14	15	16	17	18	19	20	21	22	23	24	25	26

people employed by one organization

be in the leading position on

system of ideas intended to explain something

fixed price charged for something

having a large amount of excess flesh

formal address to an audience

by every one of a group

used before the first of two alternatives

basic or inherent features of something

percentage basis

existing as a result of birth

quantity that is not a whole number

act of going to a place and returning

almost certainly

you have to find it shoes

it gives the paw to its master

it is different from one meridian to another

chemical element of atomic number 26

system of interconnected people

not easy to do when it comes to an oyster

continuous flow of liquid, air, or gas

who is waiting his turn

part connecting the head to the body.

power to provide light and heat

word used to identify

it is a pair

large, heavy, mammal

flesh of an animal as food

very large expanse of sea

laid by a female bird

we give it at the end of the riddle

up until the present

piece of cord used for fastening

the watchman must not close it

on the subject of, concerning

develop, innovate

© Dupuis Logiciels

Arrows Words 51

1	2	3	4	5	6	7	8	9	10	11	12	13
14	15	16	17	18	19	20	21	22	23	24	25	26

propel the body through water	colorless, transparent, tasteless liquid	adult human female	carry or bring with one (off)	bring about a problem or difficulty	1	2	1	3	4	preferably
5	good question to know the author	6 / 2	7	3	4	we make some casseroles	8	admired, or enjoyed by many people	2	5	9
6	10	8	2		3	move to a particular position	1	11	7	request someone to do or give
12	large quantity (1,3)	13	9		5		11		10	the condition of having paid work
13	2	3	add salt, herbs, pepper to food	3	consent to do something	14	3	
used to refer to a thing, no matter how many	2	15	16	ground adjoining a building or house	15	make a compliment to someone	2	17	4	3	3
14	2	it shines in the firmament	5	7	2	4	controlled, managed, or governed by	13
18	8	11	4	5	3	19	20	11	13	1
direction followed by a ship, road, or river	7	19	put something more	2	19	19	move suddenly and quickly	15	14
21	the way in which one acts	2	reach a place at the end of a journey	5	4	19	8
3	associated with a female person	3	13	8	22	19	3	16
10	3	4	be distant from	move at a regular and fairly slow pace	15	number of faces of a dice	5	4	13
2	forms the nucleus of a syllable	12		5	12	23	clothing for a particular purpose	3
22	22	8	6	3	14	part of the earth not covered by water	successful result in a contest	6	12	15
12	3	2	2	pass away	19	12	3	7
8	fly without moving the wings	1	14	2	15	3	direction in which a compass points	2
4	9	19	15	8	4	7	10

© Dupuis Logiciels

Arrows Words 52

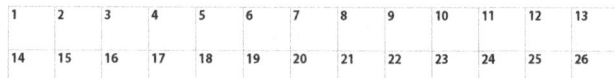

1	2	3	4	5	6	7	8	9	10	11	12	13
14	15	16	17	18	19	20	21	22	23	24	25	26

compartment for preserving food at very low temperatures.	regard as likely to happen	head of a republican state	1	2	3	4	5	1	6
7	**3**	**2**	**2**	**8**	**2**	**3**	used to express uncertainty	**9**	part of house	take charge of business	an opportunity for stating one's opinion	**5**
5	thing that is indisputably the case	**10**	do not stay on the doorstep	the wealth and resources of a country	**2**	**11**	**9**	**12**	**9**	**13**	**14**
11	newspapers or journalists viewed collectively	**1**	**3**	**2**	**6**	**6**		**13**	exchange something for something else	**5**	
15		**2**	**12**	we use it when we go out	**16**	very small	**15**	**16**	**12**	**14**	
be of the right shape and size for	reduce the amount or quantity of	**11**	**17**	**15**		**18**	**9**	**9**	**3**	**5**	situation needing to be dealt with and overcome
7	**16**	**15**	concerning all or most people	**2**		**2**	very far from the surface	**5**		**19**	
5	situated at a great distance	imposing in appearance, or style	**19**	**3**	**5**	**12**	**18**		**18**	**2**	**2**	**1**
3	**9**	**20**	**2**		**15**		fruit always green	**2**	extremely unpleasant, and degrading		**3**
it is distributed before being played	a color intermediate between green and violet	at the present time	**12**	**9**	**21**	word used to describe an action	**5**	earlier (after a measurement of time)	**5**	**19**	**9**
22	**20**	**17**	**2**			**23**	**2**	**3**	**22**	**22**	
5	behind one	people or things in a straight line	**3**	**9**	**21**		**9**		**24**	**20**	
11	from life to death		**5**	quantity obtained by multiplying	gain a point in a competitive game	**6**	**11**	**9**	**3**	**2**	**2**
25	**16**	**20**	**20**		**7**	release from captivity	**5**	fully grown female animal	**11**	**13**	
				1	**3**	**9**	**18**	**17**	**11**	**15**	
			product of five and two	**2**		**9**	lack or be short of something	**9**			
			15	**2**	**12**		**21**	**5**	**12**	**15**	

© Dupuis Logiciels

Arrows Words 53

1	2	3	4	5	6	7	8	9	10	11	12	13
14	15	16	17	18	19	20	21	22	23	24	25	26

accept his responsibilities	it allows to choose a dish	have as a consequence or result	particular kind of matter	1	2	3	4	2		introduces the second element in a comparison		thing likely to cause damage or danger
3	meet someone socially or by chance	5	6	7	8	sudden movement of surprise	9	it opposes the thought	10	6	3	2
1	6	6	used to single out one over all others	nocturnal mammal capable of flight	11	3	2	high temperature	3	choice by vote		10
1	the first one who comes	3			1		12	located a short distance away	7	6	3	4
8		7	6	13	2	nice and charming	14	small animal that has six legs		15		6
5	pay out in buying or hiring goods		1		3		7	12	9	6		3
6		1	16	6	7	17		7		9		2
person who works in a school	11	defeat the enemy	6	9	area on which a building is constructed		1	12	2		6
2	6	3	9	10	6	4	network of remote computers	6		12	he is no longer of tender age	3
not previously seen, or encountered	3		12	having the qualities required				9	15	14	8	17
1	2	4	3	7	18	6		2		7	part projecting above the mouth	8
3	not different the product of a thousand and a thousand		15	14		place a seed, bulb in the ground		11	Stendhal associated it with red		15
5	12	15	15	12	14	7		16	15	3	7	2
6		19		17		11	egg-laying vertebrate able to fly	3		14		
numerical adjective		to exchange ideas		17	12	1	9	8	1	1		
					4		20		6			
2	10	14	8	1	3	7	17					

© Dupuis Logiciels

Arrows Words 54

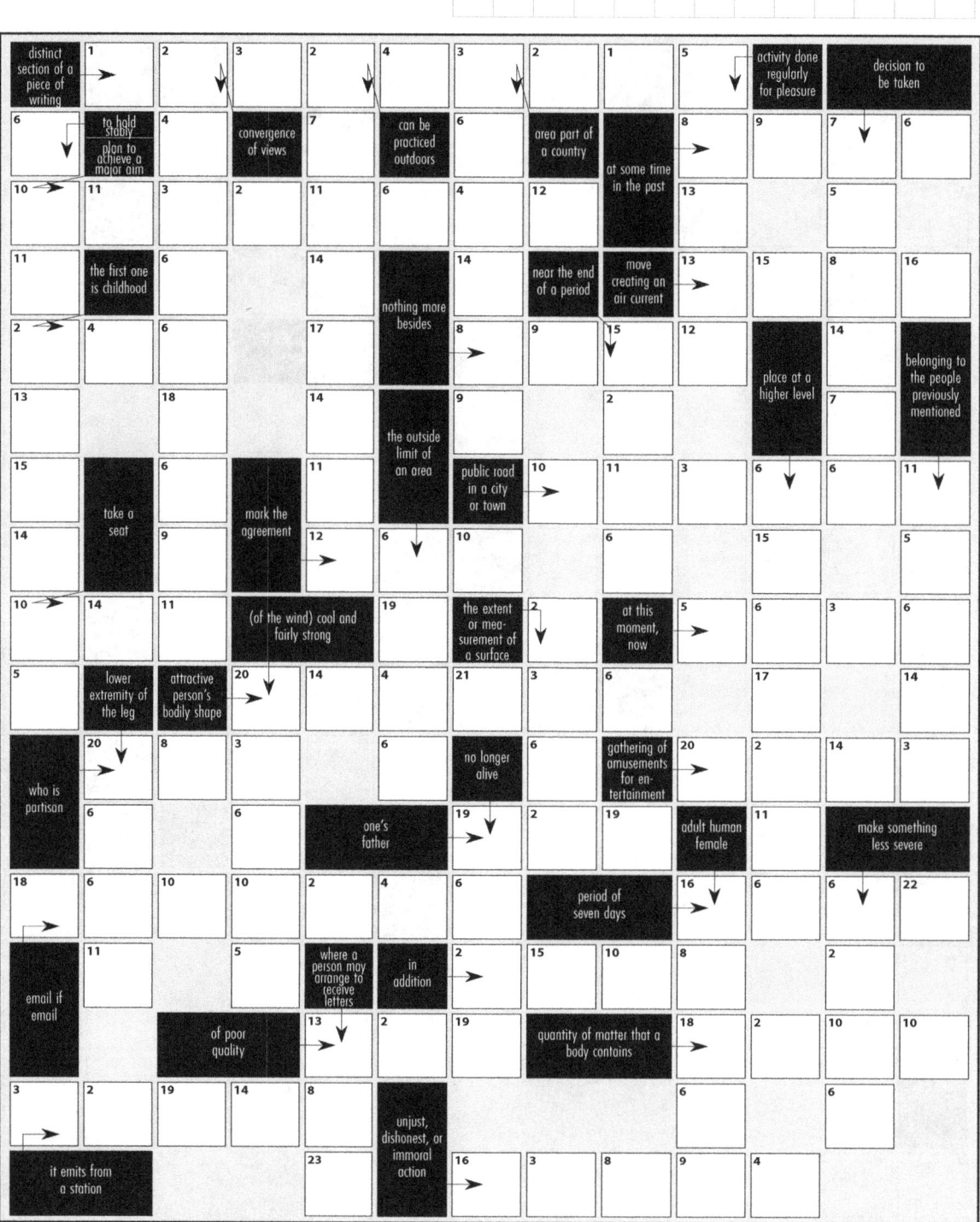

© Dupuis Logiciels

Arrows Words 55

The grid contains the following clues:

- boy in relation to his parents
- linear measure equal to one twelfth of a foot
- put or spread (something) on a surface.
- device for producing musical sounds
- set of related television programs
- get as far as
- large number of
- existing in or caused by nature
- not exposed to danger or risk
- highest in position, rank, or degree
- more than sure
- between him and me
- familiar acquiescence
- place of management of a company
- the place of the glove
- great weight
- useful to a photographer
- announce an explanation
- precious auxiliary
- it has a balance
- movements that match the rhythm of the music.
- reach in time and board
- in the direction of...
- graphite used as the part of a pencil
- Creator
- establishment providing accommodations
- he is part of the intimate
- showing physical features, cities, roads
- precedes a pronominal verb
- way people are connected
- appeal for urgent assistance

© Dupuis Logiciels

Arrows Words 56

1	2	3	4	5	6	7	8	9	10	11	12	13
14	15	16	17	18	19	20	21	22	23	24	25	26

Clues in grid:

- solid surface of the earth
- trace to disappear
- poet or musician
- excellently
- worked by electricity
- brittle substance transparent
- really
- used to indicate the existence of something
- plane figure with three sides
- it's the price you have to put
- quantity with which measures could be done
- at the highest point
- going or coming to see as a tourist
- round fruit
- space available being used by someone
- which is out of the ordinary
- part of a tree that grows out from the trunk
- the essential principles of a subject or skill
- worst is its opposite
- also (2,4)
- times a number is to be multiplied by itself
- to become a buyer
- cessation of war or violence
- between evening and morning
- for the reason that; because
- model or design used as a guide
- official record of events
- at or during the time that
- better to draw the good one
- small round portion of liquid
- the little one has just arrived
- basic cause, source, or origin of something
- be or allow to be visible
- lunch or dinner
- cut into pieces

© Dupuis Logiciels

Arrows Words 57

© Dupuis Logiciels

1	2	3	4	5	6	7	8	9	10	11	12	13
14	15	16	17	18	19	20	21	22	23	24	25	26

The grid clues include:

- we consume at this counter
- influence, or intimidation to do something.
- twelve o'clock in the day
- fictitious or true narrative or story
- arrangement to a particular sequence
- used as a neutral alternative to -man in nouns
- avoid spend money, time..
- region of the atmosphere
- a container made of flexible material
- grow in intensity
- possible choice
- achieved without great effort
- contain as part of a whole
- propane or butane
- this necessarily announces a continuation
- near
- future wife
- one hand plus two fingers
- cylindrical metal container
- person living near or next door
- smallest in amount, extent, or significance
- the last word of the tale
- to have nocturnal visions
- its detector reveals the truth
- move about in a hurried way
- ensure accuracy
- perceive with the ear
- showing stylish excellence
- less than average height
- he deals with the interests of others
- provide someone with food, or entertainment at one's own expense
- sign of operation
- keep away from
- which may be possible
- of considerable importance
- no more than, only
- society or organization

Arrows Words 58

© Dupuis Logiciels

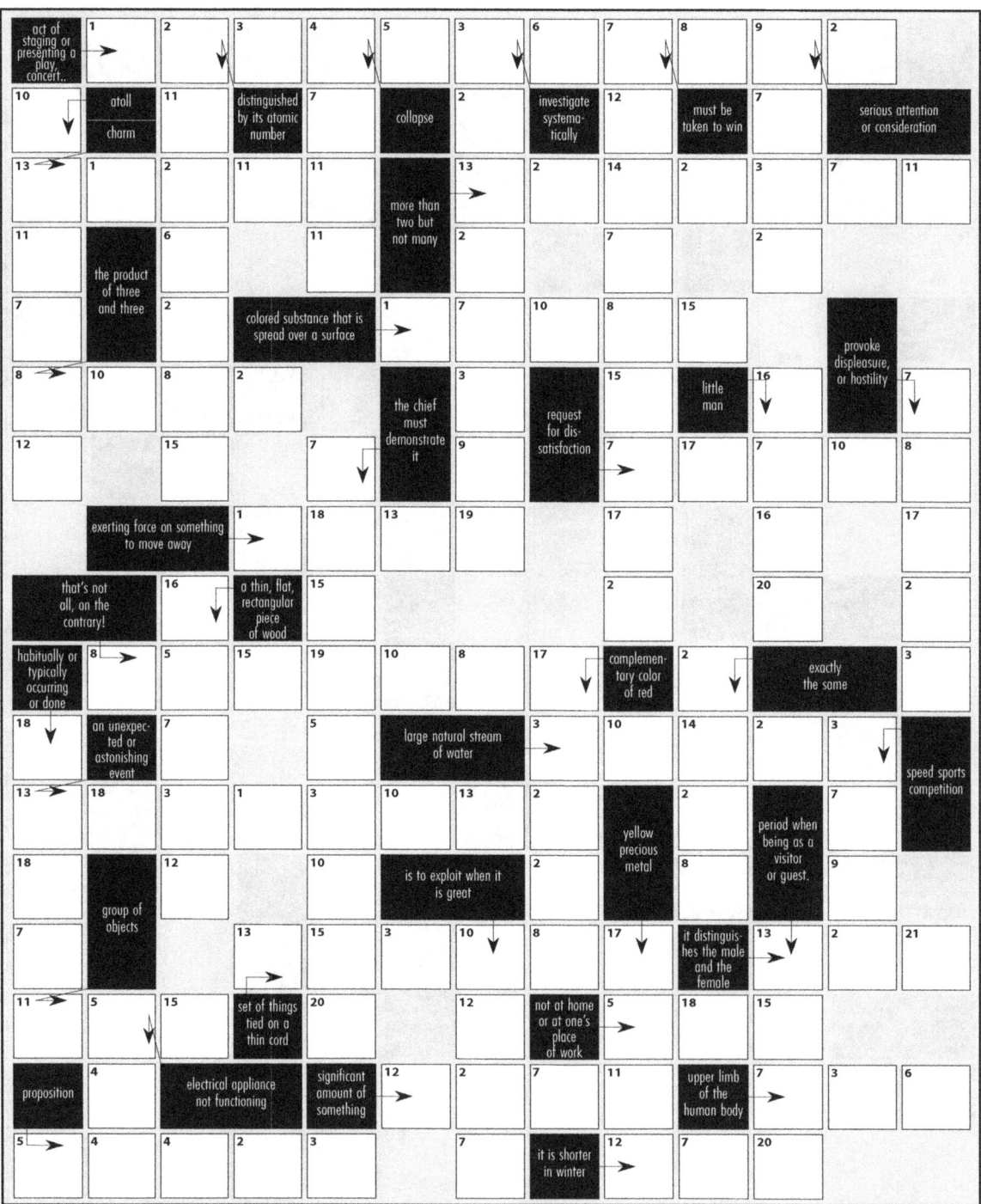

Arrows Words 59

1	2	3	4	5	6	7	8	9	10	11	12	13
14	15	16	17	18	19	20	21	22	23	24	25	26

Clues in grid:

- the remaining part of something
- be a candidate in an election
- person who is hostile
- give an account in words
- the one we are talking about
- look at written words
- extraterrestrial environment
- having the power, skill, means
- who does not joke
- sit on a horse or a bike
- state of lacking basic necessities
- the moment of the serenade
- notice the loss or absence of
- body of people with a particular purpose
- a daily printed publication
- come near or nearer
- natural disposition
- belonging to or associated with us
- resembling without being identical
- strong enough to withstand adverse conditions
- frequently
- job, occupation
- being made longer or wider without tearing or breaking
- before the expected time
- propel a ball with a bat to score runs
- group of notes sounded together
- not approximated
- used to refer to two or more people or things previously mentioned
- on the other side of a specific area
- recognize something that is difficult to detect
- armed conflict
- differ in size, amount, degree
- action, activity, event, thought

Arrows Words 60

1	2	3	4	5	6	7	8	9	10	11	12	13
14	15	16	17	18	19	20	21	22	23	24	25	26

Clues:

- number of poles
- speech or song nearly always rhythmical
- we stay there when we are sick
- set of identified individuals
- be or act as a mother or fathe
- which concerns a specific place
- of a liquid relatively firm in consistency
- control the functioning of a machine
- converse or communicate by spoken words
- welcome a visitor
- as of blood, fire, or rubies.
- covering for the foot, typically made of leather
- goes on the offensive
- people of the same age
- used to refer to all the members
- condition that someone is in at a time
- to the greatest extent
- unit of measurement of angles
- person or thing that is different
- give an infant a specified name
- bring together or into contact
- as a result or consequence of this
- label attached to a product giving its price
- only to you
- water vapor frozen into ice crystals
- in or to the place mentioned
- control your emotions (se)
- sound that is loud or unpleasant
- turn over and over on itself to form a cylinder
- continue for a specified period of time
- the way in which
- possess
- hand tool for cutting wood
- power of the mind to think, understand

© Dupuis Logiciels

ANSWERS

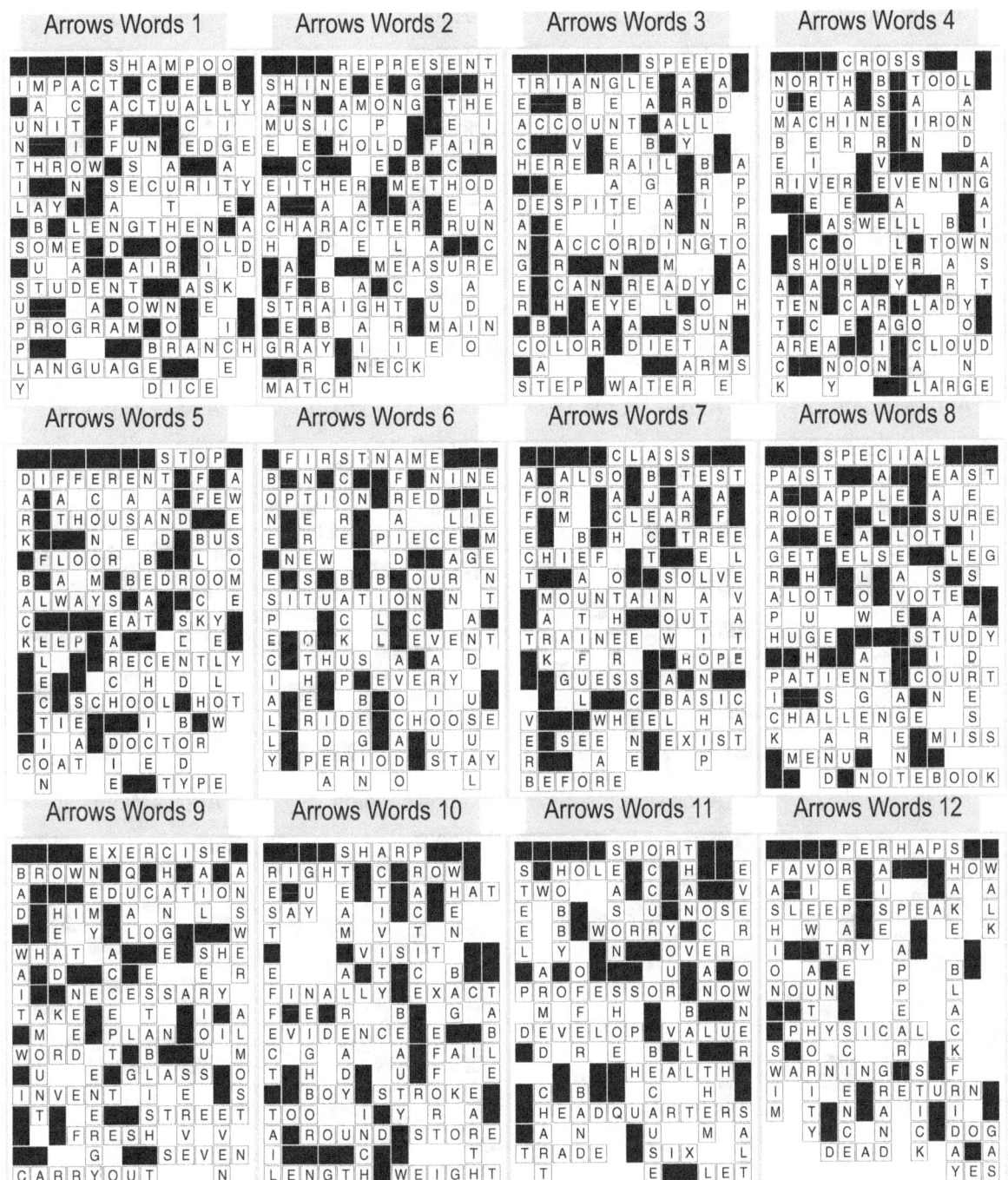

Arrows Words 1

Arrows Words 2

Arrows Words 3

Arrows Words 4

Arrows Words 5

Arrows Words 6

Arrows Words 7

Arrows Words 8

Arrows Words 9

Arrows Words 10

Arrows Words 11

Arrows Words 12

ANSWERS

Arrows Words 13

STOCK
KNOWLEDGE · A
E R E E C CRY A
Y DIVISION D
E E CNS
WAR L REDUCE
A B I A BA
L CLIMB FALSE
L A E AE HOE
RICH DRY AU
K HER
REMOVE A
E U A WORK O
PATTERN R R
E E ENGINE
AGREE X AD
T M STONE

Arrows Words 14

SPACE
PRESSURE H B
A MH C POSE
G PRIVATE PH
E L P I PI
BOX CONCERN
A Y AN DD
REMOVED B B
HOE O EXCITE
A U N IA L
I D A AT IE
B G D WHO V
MOLECULE N E
O N L
K CUT TICKET
Y Y

Arrows Words 15

FITNESS
DIFFER A A A
A A A LS V
Y CIRCLE YE
E T A S
A UNIVERSITY
PAIN O R L
P D N L
LIVE A V A
B P MILE L
PLACE I NICE
A NOTE OA
COW F QUART
K ENTER GE
E E WHY
COOKING

Arrows Words 16

GRASS
O C OPPOSITE
POST C LE H
D DIRECTION
A A A A U
DETAIL S SIGN
D O N RATE H
B T MASS N C S
CERTAIN R A
D N UNTIL F
K FIT M T F
NOR HEAVY
O EAR I B
W E O ARTICLE
SOIL E L
M L

Arrows Words 17

PITCH
E O AMERICAN
MOST I E AA
P AIR PLANET
L L B A DI
SEX FRONT IO
U ER I DN
BETWEEN VA A
J OD LEFT L
EDGE THE E
C E E ART O
T TOWARD HELP
H HC A E
SPEECH CENTER
A R E OK A
M PERSON YET
EGG K E

Arrows Words 18

INCREASE
SON A G ARMS
E CAREER C O
ALL R E HOUR
U Y E BT
SIDE HIMSELF
A E A E I A
N DURING GUN
DICE D T A I
A B SIT M
REPRESENT E A
H A A L
BROTHER ROCK
N Y C H
CREASE RECORD
U O R
ONLY COPY DAD

Arrows Words 19

SPEND A
MAGAZINE A
A B N E ANY
C CONSIDER C
H U E A TEN
I T CHURCH O
N A T L AGO
EIGHT JOY T N
A H F B B
WRITER FOLDER
E N I I AS
DESERT CAN T
D T USE K
I N JOB REPLY
N E T A
GUIDE ASK
T

Arrows Words 20

CHARACTER
RADIO C C O
E E APTITUDE
PRESS I U A A
O P T O A YOU
R B N L T
THREAT PLUG H
O A H Y RO
QUOTIENT FOUR
S N H U
REACH FINANCE
E H C DA
SHOOT SKIN
U I H DIE
L ECONOMY O
T E P SOFT
R

Arrows Words 21

CROSS
H P TRAINING
COST A F O A
O I INTEREST
S OWN E T H
MEAN R HERE
A B B A B X R
PROFESSIONAL
V DS A MA
AGE R U R PUT
A O MODEL T
IMPROVE E A
E M B T
NETWORK C
H B GA A
POPULATION C
T R N THEY

Arrows Words 22

SPOT
MOUNT H HAPPEN
A ABLE AL
TRAIN OXYGEN
C DD R C
HOME SKY PATH
I B I OR
MENTION MOVIE
A I GG RC
TEST B A
R REPUBLICAN
I A E L IC
A THERE SINCE
LI D L L
FOR OFFICIAL
N P

Arrows Words 23

SPECIAL
AFFECT S D A
C A APPLE D
CORNER E AY
O M T C B S
R A HISTORY
DEGREE A A M
I E L LIST B
N BASE L E O
G A C YARD L
T TRUTH I O
O I CREATE
AWESOME S H
H N N SEE
SHINE STOP R
C US S
SCHOOL DROP

Arrows Words 24

PARTNER
WEAR E ELSE
I E CAT A E
NOISE C DARK
E WHAT I
CHANCE SHOW
A T AGENT U
MAN P ALSO
E E MOMENT L
REAL N EAST
A R RED E
B B M WARM
LANGUAGE O V
B R C NUMBER
TYPE K T A
A ANGER
CONTINUE

ANSWERS

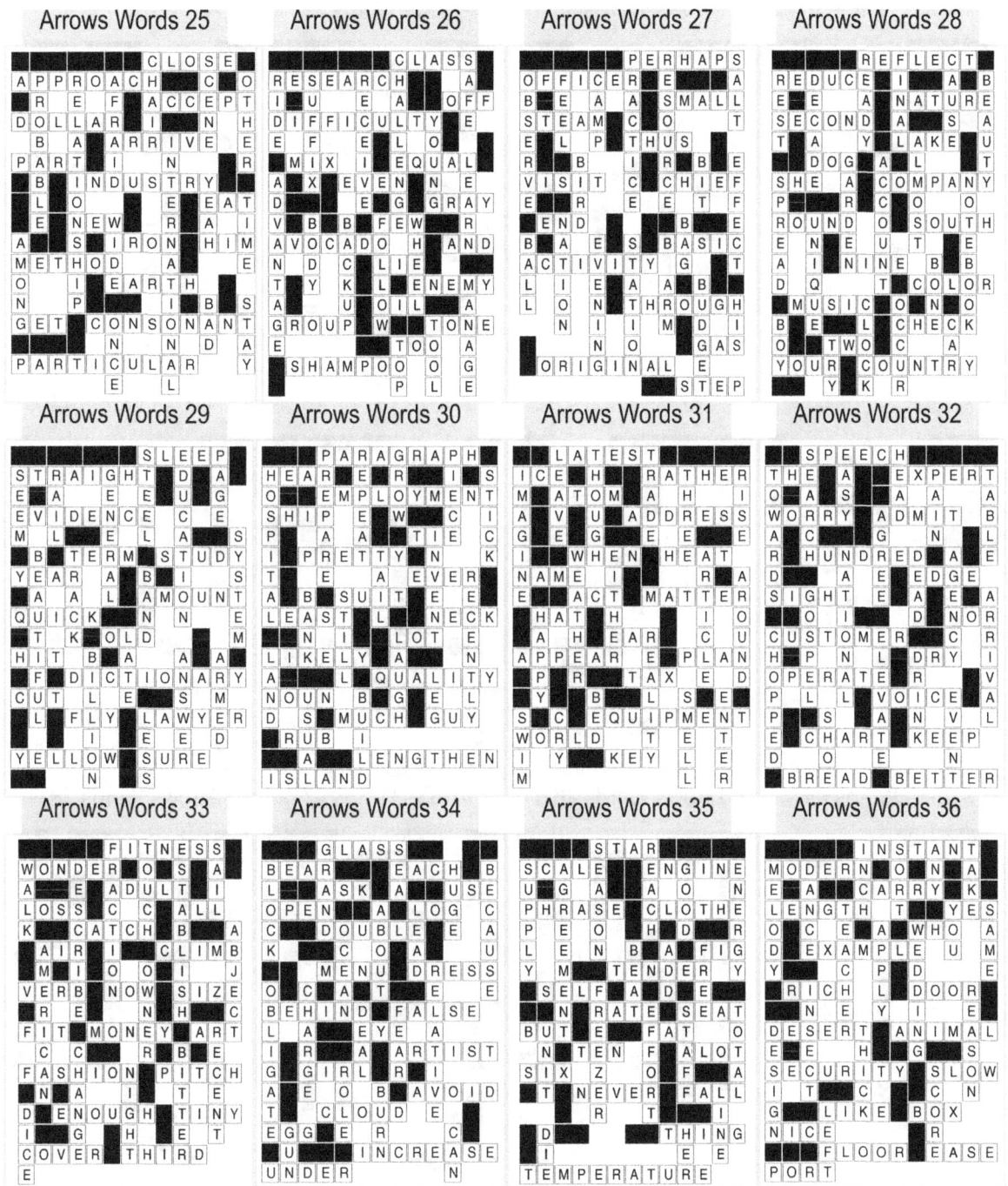

ANSWERS

ANSWERS

Arrows Words 49

Arrows Words 50

Arrows Words 51

Arrows Words 52

Arrows Words 53

Arrows Words 54

Arrows Words 55

Arrows Words 56

Arrows Words 57

Arrows Words 58

Arrows Words 59

Arrows Words 60

List of the words used in the games

3	DAY	JOY	SEA	AREA	COAT
ACT	DIE	KEY	SEE	ARMS	COOK
ADD	DOG	LAW	SET	ATOM	COPY
AGE	DRY	LAY	SEX	BABY	CORN
AGO	EAR	LEG	SHE	BACK	COST
AIR	EAT	LET	SIT	BALL	CROP
ALL	EGG	LIE	SIX	BAND	DARK
AND	END	LOG	SKY	BANK	DEAD
ANY	EYE	LOT	SON	BASE	DEAL
ARM	FAR	LOW	SUN	BEAR	DEAR
ART	FAT	MAN	TAX	BEAT	DEEP
ASK	FEW	MAP	TEN	BELL	DICE
BAD	FIG	MAY	THE	BEST	DIET
BAG	FIT	MIX	TIE	BILL	DOOR
BAR	FLY	NEW	TOO	BIRD	DOWN
BAT	FOR	NOR	TOP	BLOW	DRAW
BED	FUN	NOW	TRY	BLUE	DROP
BIG	GAS	OFF	TWO	BOAT	EACH
BIT	GET	OIL	USE	BODY	EASE
BOX	GUN	OLD	WAR	BONE	EAST
BOY	GUY	OUR	WHO	BOOK	EASY
BUS	HAT	OUT	WHY	BORN	EDGE
BUT	HER	OWN	WIN	BOTH	ELSE
BUY	HIM	PAY	YES	BURN	EVEN
CAN	HIS	PUT	YET	CALL	EVER
CAR	HIT	RED	YOU	CAMP	FACE
CAT	HOT	ROW		CARD	FACT
COW	HOW	RUB		CARE	FAIL
CRY	ICE	RUN	**4**	CASE	FAIR
CUT	INN	SAW	ABLE	CELL	FALL
DAD	JOB	SAY	ALOT	CENT	FARM
			ALSO		

List of the words used in the games

FEAR	HOME	MEAN	PLUG	SAVE	TAIL
FEED	HOUR	MEAT	POEM	SEAT	TAKE
FEEL	HUGE	MENU	POOR	SEED	TALE
FEET	IDEA	MILE	PORT	SEEM	TALK
FISH	INCH	MISS	POSE	SELF	TALL
FLAT	IRON	MORE	POST	SEND	TASK
FOOT	JUMP	MOST	PUSH	SHIP	TEAM
FOUR	KEEP	MUCH	RACE	SHOE	TERM
FREE	KILL	NAME	RAIL	SHOP	TEST
FROM	KIND	NEAR	RAIN	SHOW	THAN
GAME	KING	NECK	RATE	SIDE	THAT
GIRL	KNOW	NEED	READ	SIGN	THEM
GIVE	LADY	NEXT	REAL	SITE	THEN
GLAD	LAKE	NICE	REST	SIZE	THEY
GOAL	LAND	NINE	RICH	SKIN	THUS
GOLD	LAST	NOON	RIDE	SLIP	TIME
GOOD	LATE	NOSE	RISE	SLOW	TINY
GRAY	LEAD	NOTE	RISK	SNOW	TONE
GROW	LEFT	NOUN	ROAD	SOFT	TOOL
HAIR	LESS	ONCE	ROCK	SOIL	TOWN
HALF	LIKE	ONLY	ROLE	SOME	TREE
HAND	LINE	OPEN	ROLL	SOON	TRIP
HARD	LIST	OVER	ROOM	SORT	TRUE
HAVE	LIVE	PAGE	ROOT	SPOT	TUBE
HEAD	LOSE	PAIN	ROPE	STAR	TYPE
HEAR	LOSS	PART	RULE	STAY	UNIT
HEAT	LOUD	PAST	SAFE	STEP	VARY
HELP	MAIN	PATH	SAIL	STOP	VERB
HERE	MANY	PICK	SALT	SUIT	VERY
HOLD	MARK	PLAN	SAME	SURE	VIEW
HOLE	MASS	PLAY	SAND	SWIM	VOTE

List of the words used in the games

WAIT
WALK
WALL
WANT
WARM
WEAR
WEEK
WHAT
WHEN
WIDE
WORD
WORK
YARD
YEAH
YEAR
YOUR

5

ABOUT
ABOVE
ADMIT
ADULT
AFTER
AGAIN
AGENT
AGREE
ALLOW
AMONG
ANGER
APPLE
APPLY

ARMED
AVOID
BASIC
BEGIN
BLACK
BLOCK
BOARD
BREAD
BRING
BROWN
BUILD
CARRY
CATCH
CAUSE
CHAIR
CHART
CHECK
CHIEF
CHORD
CLASS
CLEAR
CLIMB
CLOCK
CLOSE
CLOUD
COACH
COAST
COLOR
COURT
COVER

CROSS
DANCE
DEATH
DREAM
DRESS
DRINK
EARLY
EARTH
EIGHT
ENEMY
ENTER
EQUAL
EVENT
EVERY
EXACT
EXIST
FALSE
FAVOR
FIELD
FINAL
FIRST
FLOOR
FRESH
FRONT
GLASS
GRAND
GRASS
GREAT
GREEN
GROUP
GUESS

GUIDE
HAPPY
HEART
HEAVY
HOBBY
HORSE
HOUSE
LARGE
LAUGH
LEARN
LEAST
LEAVE
LEVEL
LOCAL
MATCH
METAL
MODEL
MONEY
MONTH
MOUNT
MOVIE
MUSIC
NEVER
NIGHT
NOISE
NORTH
OCCUR
OCEAN
OFFER
OFTEN

ORDER
ORGAN
OTHER
OWNER
PAINT
PAPER
PEACE
PHONE
PIECE
PITCH
PLACE
PLAIN
PLANE
PLANT
POINT
POWER
PRESS
QUART
QUICK
RADIO
RAISE
RANGE
REACH
READY
REPLY
RIGHT
RIVER
ROUND
SCALE
SCENE
SCORE

SERVE
SEVEN
SHAKE
SHARP
SHEET
SHINE
SHOOT
SIGHT
SINCE
SLAVE
SLEEP
SMALL
SMELL
SOLVE
SOUTH
SPACE
SPEAK
SPEED
SPELL
SPEND
SPORT
STAFF
STAIN
STAND
START
STATE
STEAM
STEEL
STICK
STILL
STOCK

List of the words used in the games

STONE	WATER	ATTACK	DECIDE	IMPACT
STORE	WHEEL	AUTHOR	DEGREE	INSECT
STORY	WHERE	BACKUP	DESERT	INVENT
STUDY	WHICH	BEAUTY	DESIGN	ISLAND
TABLE	WOMAN	BEFORE	DETAIL	LATEST
TEACH	WOMEN	BEHIND	DIFFER	LAWYER
THANK	WORLD	BETTER	DINNER	LENGTH
THEIR	WORRY	BITTER	DOCTOR	LIKELY
THERE	WRONG	BRANCH	DOLLAR	LISTEN
THICK	YOUNG	BRIGHT	DOUBLE	LITTLE
THING		BUDGET	DURING	MAGNET
THIRD		CAMERA	EFFECT	MANAGE
THREE	**6**	CAREER	EFFORT	MATTER
THROW	ABJECT	CENTER	EITHER	MELODY
TODAY	ACCEPT	CHANCE	ENERGY	METHOD
TOTAL	ACTION	CHANGE	ENGINE	MODERN
TOUCH	AFFECT	CHARGE	ENOUGH	MOMENT
TOUGH	AFRAID	CHOICE	EXCITE	NATION
TRACK	AGENCY	CHOOSE	EXPECT	NATURE
TRADE	ALMOST	CHURCH	EXPERT	NOTICE
TRAIN	ALWAYS	CIRCLE	FIGURE	NUMBER
TREAT	AMOUNT	CLOTHE	FOLDER	OFFICE
TRUTH	ANIMAL	COLONY	FOLLOW	OPTION
UNDER	ANSWER	CORNER	FRIEND	OTHERS
UNTIL	APPEAR	COUPLE	GARDEN	OXYGEN
USUAL	AROUND	COURSE	GATHER	PARENT
VALUE	ARRIVE	CREASE	GOSPEL	PEOPLE
VISIT	ARTIST	CREATE	GROUND	PERIOD
VOICE	ASSUME	DANGER	HAPPEN	PERMIT
VOWEL	ASWELL	DECADE	HEALTH	PERSON

List of the words used in the games

PHRASE	STRONG	BEDROOM	FREEZER	PROBLEM
PLANET	SUFFIX	BELIEVE	GENERAL	PROCESS
PRETTY	SUPPLY	BETWEEN	HIMSELF	PRODUCT
RATHER	SYMBOL	BILLION	HISTORY	PROGRAM
REASON	SYSTEM	BLANKET	HUNDRED	QUALITY
RECENT	TENDER	BROTHER	IMAGINE	REALITY
RECORD	THEORY	CERTAIN	IMPROVE	RECEIVE
REDUCE	THOUGH	CHOPPED	INCLUDE	REFLECT
REGION	THREAT	COMPANY	INSTANT	REMOVED
REMOVE	TICKET	CONCERN	MACHINE	SCIENCE
REPEAT	TOWARD	CONNECT	MEASURE	SECTION
REPORT	TWENTY	CONTAIN	MENTION	SERIOUS
RESULT	UNIQUE	CONTROL	MESSAGE	SEVERAL
RETURN	VALLEY	COOKING	MILLION	SHAMPOO
SCHOOL	WEAPON	COUNTRY	NATURAL	SIMILAR
SEARCH	WEIGHT	DESPITE	NETWORK	SPECIAL
SEASON	WONDER	DEVELOP	NOTHING	STATION
SECOND	WRITER	DISCUSS	NUMERAL	STRANGE
SELECT	YELLOW	DISEASE	OBSERVE	STRETCH
SENIOR		ECONOMY	OFFICER	STUDENT
SERIES	**7**	ELEMENT	OPERATE	SUBJECT
SIMPLE	ACCOUNT	ELEVATE	PARTNER	SUPPORT
SINGLE	ADDRESS	EVENING	PATIENT	SURFACE
SOCIAL	AGAINST	EXAMPLE	PATTERN	TEACHER
SPEECH	ALREADY	FASHION	PERHAPS	THOUGHT
SPREAD	ARRIVAL	FEDERAL	POPULAR	THROUGH
STREAM	ARTICLE	FEELING	POSTMAN	TOWARDS
STREET	AVOCADO	FINALLY	PREPARE	TRAINEE
STRING	AWESOME	FINANCE	PRESENT	VARIOUS
STROKE	BECAUSE	FITNESS	PRIVATE	VILLAGE

List of the words used in the games

WARNING · INTEREST · STRAIGHT · PROFESSOR

WEATHER · LANGUAGE · STRATEGY · REPRESENT

WEDDING · LENGTHEN · SURPRISE · RIGHTHERE

MAGAZINE · SYLLABLE · SITUATION

8

MATERIAL · THOUSAND · SOMETIMES

ACTIVITY · MILITARY · TOGETHER · STRUCTURE

ACTUALLY · MOLECULE · TRAINING · SUBSTANCE

AMERICAN · MOUNTAIN · TRIANGLE

APPROACH · MOVEMENT

10

APTITUDE · NATIONAL

9

DICTIONARY

BEHAVIOR · NEIGHBOR · ADVANTAGE · DIFFICULTY

BLACKOUT · NOTEBOOK · AGREEMENT · EMPLOYMENT

BUSINESS · OBLIGATE · AUTHORITY · ESPECIALLY

CAMPAIGN · OFFICIAL · BEAUTIFUL · GENERATION

CARRYOUT · OPPOSITE · CANDIDATE · INSTRUMENT

CONSIDER · ORIGINAL · CHALLENGE · PARTICULAR

CONTINUE · PHYSICAL · CHARACTER · POPULATION

CULTURAL · PLEASANT · CONSONANT · REPUBLICAN

CUSTOMER · PRACTICE · DIFFERENT · UNIVERSITY

DESCRIBE · PRESSURE · DIRECTION

11

DIVISION · PROBABLE · EDUCATION · ACCORDINGTO

ELECTION · PROBABLY · EQUIPMENT · BLACKFRIDAY

ELECTRIC · QUOTIENT · ESTABLISH · ENVIRONMENT

EVIDENCE · RECENTLY · FIRSTNAME · INFORMATION

EXERCISE · RELATIVE · FOREIGNER · INSTITUTION

FRACTION · RESEARCH · KNOWLEDGE · PERFORMANCE

HOSPITAL · RESOURCE · NECESSARY · TEMPERATURE

INCREASE · SECURITY · NEWSPAPER

12

INDICATE · SENTENCE · PARAGRAPH · HEADQUARTERS

INDUSTRY · SHOULDER · PRESIDENT · ORGANIZATION

PROFESSIONAL

RELATIONSHIP

13

INTERNATIONAL

14

ADMINISTRATION

92086897R00039